SMALL

ON

PURPOSE

Praise for *Small on Purpose*

"*Small on Purpose* was written by a pastor with deep compassion for churches of less than one hundred members who faithfully gather each week, energized by the Spirit. Parks gives readers, both clergy and laity, a new framework for considering these churches as sufficient and significant spaces for God's work to occur in worship, pastoral care, and being church. Read and take hope!"

—Robin Knowles Wallace, Professor in the Taylor Endowed Chair of Worship and Music, Methodist Theological School in Ohio, Delaware, OH

"*Small on Purpose* reimagines what it means to be a congregation of ninety, sixty, or thirty by not focusing on size. I especially appreciate Lewis Parks's attention to why 'soul care' is critical for congregations under 150 as a means of discipleship and outreach. Parks sees soul care as a countercultural act that creates meaning for many who are seeking family-like relationships. This book challenges all congregations to take seriously the small things they are doing— like soul care—as a compelling way to move into the future."

—F. Douglas Powe Jr., Managing Director for The Institute for Community Engagement, Wesley Theological Seminary, Washington, DC; author of *New Wine, New Wineskins* and *Not Safe for Church* from Abingdon Press

"Lewis Parks writes with pitch-perfect tone about the life of small churches. He appeals to the experience of smaller congregations as gathering places of worship and service. There he sees signs of the Spirit moving, of tradition revivified through song and word, of pastoral care shared across a congregation. Above all, he offers transformative words and perspectives with which small churches can claim their distinctive witness."

—Thomas Edward Frank, University Professor and Chair of the Department of History, Wake Forest College, Wake Forest University, Winston-Salem, NC

"In a time when the culture is becoming more and more individualistic, Lew Parks strikes a chord for the great value of the gathered community of faith that is strengthened week by week through their faithfulness to the gospel and to one another. Gather in your small church and read this together. Your life and your community will be enriched."

—Bill McAlilly, Bishop, Nashville Episcopal Area of The United Methodist Church

"Dr. Parks candidly presents both challenges and deep rewards of ministry in churches that are *Small on Purpose*. Since dramatic changes uproot old assumptions about ministry, it is extremely helpful to have fresh guidance from a proven mentor, teacher, and scholar, who is also currently shepherding a small church. Seamlessly integrated into his warm and down-to-earth writing is Dr. Parks's theological depth rooted in scripture and theology."

—Gil Waldkoenig, Professor of Church in Society, Gettysburg Seminary, Gettysburg, Pennsylvania

SMALL

ON PURPOSE

Life in a Significant Church

Lewis A. Parks

Nashville

SMALL ON PURPOSE:
LIFE IN A SIGNIFICANT CHURCH

Copyright © 2017 by Abingdon Press

This book is printed on acid-free paper.

Library of Congress Cataloging-in-Publication Data has been requested.

ISBN: 978-1-5018-2732-7

17 18 19 20 21 22 23 24 25 26—10 9 8 7 6 5 4 3 2 1
MANUFACTURED IN THE UNITED STATES OF AMERICA

To Calvary of Lemoyne and small churches everywhere:
that they might know their worth

CONTENTS

Contents

INTRODUCTION

It's eight thirty Sunday morning, and I am sitting at the stop sign waiting to get out of our neighborhood onto Lisburn Road to begin my ten-mile commute to the small church where I serve as pastor. I am waiting for a break in the traffic that is headed in the same direction, toward the megachurch (average attendance 3,500) that sits in the middle of an eighty-five-acre plot of rolling farmland about a mile from my house.

Sometimes there is no pause in the traffic for ten minutes—lots of time for me to brood and imagine. I swear, all the cars are newer SUVs with young parents and two or more children. Everyone looks happy. And why shouldn't they? The seats they will soon occupy will be theatre seats with cup holders. (The foam in the cushions of our pews dried out when the first Bush was president. Bring your own cushion!) The smiling families of the megachurch will be mesmerized by professional musicians, moved and educated by an attractive preacher. They will hear an incredible menu of holistic opportunities available to them in the coming week.

1

Large churches and megachurches now account for 50 percent of Christian worshippers on Sunday morning. These churches are on the forefront of reaching a younger and more diverse population. I especially appreciate that they have the capacity and the constituency that affords them a voice in the public market space, and I truly do root for them.

At the same time, I envy them. They've got the buildings, grounds, and parking. They've got the young families with children. They've got stunning points of entry like a sports complex rivaling that of a small college and concerts by well-known Christian performers. They've got the people, the favor of the public and of the denomination; they've got the momentum.

What have we got? We, the leaders and the people of a small church struggling with an old oversized building, desperate for children, youth, and young adults, demographically challenged, confronting our limits whichever way we turn, making do, getting by—what have we got?

That is the question of this book. I begin the search with an exercise in imagination that asks us to forget much of what we think we know about small churches so that we may receive fresh impressions (chapter 1). Then I turn to the two most important things small churches do: they gather weekly to worship God from the wellspring of their native religious creativity (chapter 2), and they sustain a community of soul care (chapter 3).

Next we turn to a neglected subject in the study of small churches: their capacity to order their lives, to organize and define themselves in better ways, such as "dynamic equilibrium," that will generate confidence (chapter 4). I challenge some of the dismissive thinking about small churches and their buildings in chapter 5 and then present a case study of an all-too-common situation: a small church in an oversized building. Then we finish with some hard questions hanging in the air above small churches today such as, "How serious can you be with a part-time pastor?" (chapter 6).

Without apology, this is a journey slowed down by theological reflection. It is also a journey where I frequently shut up and point. Sometimes I will be pointing at Calvary United Methodist Church in Lemoyne, Pennsylvania. Theirs is not a "turnaround" story, at least not yet. Theirs is a story of a church struggling to find its worth during a season of doubt. Above all else, they and the 270,000 congregations about their size need to recover a sense of their own significance before God. I want to help.

Chapter 1

AN EXERCISE IN SELECTIVE AMNESIA

W hat if you as pastor-in-charge woke up one Sunday morning with a case of selective amnesia? You remember enough to eat your breakfast, shower, and feed the family pets. You check your e-mail, give a quick "see you later" kiss to your spouse, and drive to the congregation of ninety, or sixty, or thirty souls you lead. You arrive thirty minutes before the gathering music. And somewhere between the car and the front steps of the church the selective amnesia sets in.

You do not remember the rhetoric of mainline decline. It's not only the facts behind the rhetoric that escape you—the decreased numbers of membership and worship attendance, the absence of younger generations, the outdated and oversized buildings, and so on—but the rhetoric itself, the embellished, argumentative, phrase mongering use of those facts to diss present forms of the church and offer new products in their place.

You do not remember that this form of organizing life together as a people, this church, has been variously criticized as outdated, inflexible, racist, classist, out-of-touch, isolationist, and in denial of its own imminent and certain death.

There's another rhetoric slipping from memory this morning, the rhetoric of post-Christian America. Nobody is sure when that "post" began. Was there some sort of pristine colonial America height from which we have been falling ever since? Is the decline synonymous with the rise and decline of that uniquely American form of connection of churches called a denomination? Did the fall begin on a Sunday evening in 1963 when the Fox movie theatre in Greenville, South Carolina, started to show movies in head-to-head competition with the youth group meeting at the Buncombe Street Methodist Church?[1]

Whenever that "post" began, the corresponding rhetoric goes something like this. "You are no longer the dominant voice in social laws and customs you once were—deal with it!" "You are not above scrutiny and liability for the way you have and do hurt individuals." "Your claim to superior religious truth no longer has favored status; you are in level-field competition with other religions, cults, and a growing preference for a world without interference from any sort of god." As potent and pervasive as that rhetoric may be, it is erased from your memory this morning, gone without a trace.

Gone with it is the memory of a marketplace logic that bigger is better. You do not remember that within a span of fifty years the smaller community schools were swept away by large regional campuses and it was called good; that small specialty businesses were swallowed by big-box chain stores and it was called good; or that television channel options exploded from the basic four

(ABC, CBS, NBC, and PBS) to hundreds and it was called good. Or that such developments and their counterparts in the church growth movement (consolidation, convenience, options) were declared very good.

There are certainly other marketplace logics like the logic of a small business where you maintain certain values alongside the profit motive or the logic of sustaining a dynamic equilibrium in an organization, but most days these logics are eclipsed by the "bigger is better" scenario. And in this setting your congregation of ninety, sixty, or thirty is like a passenger who lost her ticket to ride, an office manager left behind because he missed the memo about an important meeting. It is the specter of being displaced that haunts you some days. But not today. Today you have a temporary reprieve from that memory.

On this day, you cannot for the life of you remember a single one of those "life cycle of a congregation" charts comparing your congregation to the one-way ascent, peak, and descent of an individual person and locating your congregation at various points along the downward slope to death. So you are not prone to dismiss your repeat pattern of worship as creeping middle age, your investment in the right ordering of life together as the onset of poor health, or the keeping of certain persons with certain gifts in office as the rise of an end-times aristocracy. The all-too-easy comparisons between the lifespan of a human being (in the United States, eighty-four years for men, eighty-six for women)[2] to the lifespan of small tenacious congregations (routinely one hundred to two hundred years) are forgotten this morning.

Forgotten also are all those caricatures of small churches you have accumulated through the years. Caricature: "A representation in which the subject's distinctive features or peculiarities are exaggerated for comic or grotesque effect."[3] So you do not remember your congregation as a dysfunctional family system plagued by symptoms of poor communication, codependent personality disorders, or a tendency to pounce on scapegoats. You do not remember remarks by a denominational official or consultant hired by that official that small churches are a "drag to the system," demanding supervisory time and leadership resources far out of proportion to their contribution to the larger connection of churches. And most of all you do not remember the false memory of nostalgia, an idealized image of the past that exchanges vague emotions of misty-eyed longing—think "There's a Church in the Valley by the Wildwood" with its complete absence of God-talk—for the plain courage to face present challenges.

Add to the list of things forgotten the economics of scarcity surrounding your financial support. You are given a respite from the constant tension of whether this congregation is a viable economic unit as measured by its capacity to sustain your base salary, health insurance, and pension. You forget their injured confidence born in a series of defensive moves over forty years: from pastoral staff to solo pastor, from solo pastor to solo pastor of lesser credential, from solo pastor of lesser credential to pastor shared with another congregation, and from shared pastor full-time to shared pastor part-time.

How does a congregation scale back its self-worth in keeping with such a descent in the status of its leadership? Is it less church under the shared pastor part-time than it was under the staff that led in the same building forty years ago? This morning, for a few minutes, you are spared these questions that dog your ordinary working days. You are spared as well their counterpart in your psyche, those two nagging questions that can quickly deflate best intentions of pastoral leadership and compassion. *How long can they afford me? How long can I afford to stay with them?*

And one more thing: this morning you do not remember the sting of career competition. You forget that hideous little voice of doubt that asks, "Is this really the rung of the ladder I should be occupying at this stage of my life?" You forget the mental ranking, the envious gazes at larger congregations with imagined perks, and the anxious comparing to colleagues, especially those younger. By a temporary loss of select memory, you are at the right church at the right time, the congregation worthy of your best efforts.

You park your car in the well-worn lot, enter through the heavy double doors painted fire engine red, and gaze around without the baggage jettisoned by your amnesia but with the curious and sympathetic eye of an explorer. What do you see?

A frail gentleman maybe in his sixties, an obvious victim of multiple strokes, sits in the last pew long before others gather, as if seeking a private audience with God to sort out the collapse of his active life narrative.

The front of the sanctuary is adorned in festive red with occasional white doves like a stadium draped with team colors. Soon there will be ushers, acolytes, pastor, and people in the pews sporting that color reinforcing the message that the spirit of God is poured out generously, abundantly, extravagantly upon even this particular gathering of ninety, sixty, or thirty persons.

People gather. About two-thirds are over sixty, but the smattering of young adults and children are known to all by name and will have active roles in the sixty minutes of drama to follow. It is obvious from the constant chatter before and after the service and during the "passing of the peace" that these persons are engaged with one another's stories.

People worship. People sing to God "immortal, invisible" and invite that God to interrupt their everyday preoccupations through acts of prayer, singing, witness, offering, and sacrament. People submit to God "unresting, unhasting" their weekday rhythms and races in exchange for glimpses of the slower but sure work of providence. People wait expectantly for God, "the true life of all," to speak a plain word through the scriptures and the preacher. People imagine and rehearse before God "almighty, victorious" the final end of their souls and of this world.[4]

And then the people scatter. Some of them will see each other at the Sunday school hour, or the Monday evening meetings. A core will regroup for the midweek meal for the community, or the Thursday choir practice, but most will not see each other until they gather again on Sunday. This is not a 24/7 church. It does not have the resources to sustain a comprehensive counterculture. Nor does it have the will. It is enough that the people scatter to their spheres of influence—significant others, families, schools, jobs, callings, environments—changed and better equipped to do good and not do harm.

So the people gather, worship, and scatter with a blessing "in the name of the Father, Son, and Holy Spirit." And here's the thing: it will happen over and over again, ninety, sixty, or thirty people, week after week, "maintaining" worship. It is a phenomenon worthy of respect, before it is a symptom screaming for diagnosis. Something significant is happening here. It was happening before you were their pastor and will continue after you are gone.

You may add or take away from the vitality while you are there, but this organism clearly has a source of energy apart from you.

⌒—

The effective pastor of a small church must seek words for the phenomena before him or her, words that release native energy rather than censor it. That means moving beyond mere statistics: the ninety, sixty, or thirty average worship attendance; the weekly giving; the average age that tells one story to the harder-to-quantify character of the soul of the congregation which may tell a different story. That pastor knows the mesmerizing power of idealized projections, what Dietrich Bonhoeffer so accurately describes as the "wish dreams" that get in the way of life together in a small faith community. The pastor will surrender those wish dreams, not for some disarmed, dismantled, or decommissioned "true" version (that, too, is a projection that may say more about the subject than the object), but for a better version of the church as drawing its vitality, intrigue, and significance from a source outside itself. "Not an Ideal but Divine Reality," says Bonhoeffer.[5] It is a way of reminding us that the reality therapy of overcoming our wish dreams is not the destination, but only a preparation for the journey toward real church. We will need to look elsewhere to be equipped for that journey.

Naming Church

Pastors who have been to seminary or taken an extended course of study pick up a specialist language called theology. It is a type of shoptalk, words and acronyms they throw around with other pastors. Most of the words are drawn from distant times and places—words like *ecclesia* (an ancient Greek New Testament word for church), *reformation* (a movement in the sixteenth-century church of Europe), *prevenient grace* (a theological term found in the eighteenth-century sermons of John Wesley), or *Q* (a hypothetical collection of the sayings of Jesus first named by early twentieth-century German biblical scholars). Some of the shop-talk is of more recent vintage, words like *missional church, narrative theology,* or *mainline decline.* A fair amount of this shoptalk (theology), past and present, is related to the nature and mission of the church (ecclesiology).

To learn the language of theology in general and ecclesiology in particular is to be equipped to see things missed by most others. This language never was intended to be mere shoptalk, an esoteric language by which we on the inside take pleasure in distinguishing ourselves from those on the outside. This language was intended to open worlds by injecting names into the dense flow of experience—names that make shadowy forms come forward into the light of day, reveal thunderous energy beneath a placid surface, and release fresh experiences in what was assumed to be a used-up landscape.

To say "God" is to disrupt any comfortable view of the world that excludes a divine origin, source, and end. Either you take back the word or you begin to look for data that disconfirms a closed secular worldview. To say "God" is to insist that there is more than meets our eyes. When Jesus says, "God is spirit, and it is necessary to worship God in spirit and truth" (John 4:24), he is pointing not only to our final destination but also to the *more* in our midst now.

In a similar way ecclesiology points to the more in our midst now. To talk about the marks of the true church, the biblical names for the church, the Great Commission, governance in the church, missional church, or any of the terms in a generous repertoire provided for the church in its scriptures and in its reflection on those scriptures in theology is to make counterclaims to a reduced visibility reading of the local congregation.

The Gifts of the Spirit to Every Church of Any Size

A case in point: the Bible and the church's teachings make certain claims about the presence and effectiveness of the spirit of God in the local congregation. There is a consensus that these claims apply to every congregation of every time, place, and size. There is neither more nor less reach of the Spirit in the congregation of ninety, sixty, or thirty than there is in a congregation of two thousand. There is neither more nor less pressure being exercised by the Spirit upon congregations in the older centers of Christianity like Europe or North America than in the newer centers like Africa or South America. The Spirit holds nothing back from your small congregation in rural Kansas. And the Spirit brings it all to my small congregation in an urban setting of Pennsylvania.

There is also consensus on what these gifts of the Spirit to the local congregation are: (1) the Spirit creates the congregation from diverse persons; (2) the Spirit makes God present in the worship; (3) the Spirit gives to the congregation every spiritual gift it needs; and (4) the Spirit seeks to reform and revive the congregation.[6]

As the resident theologian of my congregation, I travel back and forth from the church's texts (Bible and theology) and the local congregation. To the texts I carry the wearisome and worrisome details of congregational life. The sinkholes in the parking lot are getting deeper, and there is no money to repair. One of our three active young adults has been diagnosed with a health issue. The narcotics anonymous group is discarding their cigarette butts on the steps. Such realities challenge the lofty claims of the texts, threatening to dismiss them as inflated, idealistic, or out of touch.

To the local congregation I carry the claims of the texts as afterimages, vivid impressions that linger after leaving the pages of Paul's letter to the Philippians or Moltmann's *The Church in the Power of the Spirit.* These afterimages build expectation that there is more to the local congregation than its wearisome and worrisome details. At a minimum they hint at what else should/could/may be going on there. In the instance of the Spirit's gifts to the churches, it creates a climate of expectation. Who knows? The gray heron may show. The fourth moon of Jupiter may be spotted. The rookie may have a breakout game. The effective presence of God, the Holy Spirit, may manifest itself as energy, attraction, inspiration, conviction, resolve, and encouragement. If only I will attend to what is in front of me.

The Spirit Creates the Congregation from Diverse Persons

The Spirit attracts to this group persons who would not naturally seek out one another. The Spirit may cooperate with other forces of attraction: family ties, community ties, or the homogeneous principle that people prefer to become Christians without crossing barriers of kin, race, or class. But the Spirit does not stop there and in fact seems to take delight in bringing together and holding together those who are not "our kind." There is a divine energy at work sustaining a unified life together: "one Lord, one faith, one baptism" (Eph 4:5). And the Spirit does this by soliciting persons who may come from remarkably different backgrounds and stories.

Even in the smallest of congregations that energy is at work. Sitting in the same pew or row of chairs may be found the homeless person and the person with a six-figure salary; the heroin addict trying to come clean and the adult with no known health risk factors; representatives from four very different generations; the highly educated and the minimally educated; those who are well traveled and the stay-at-homes; those who are tech savvy and those who are not.

Todd was the first person in our congregation to discover that a certain video game app was using our church sign as a targeted area. Imagine the honor! We had become a PokéStop for the video game *Pokémon Go*. There are less than ten others in the congregation who could take pleasure in Todd's discovery, who get the attraction of fast, interactive games on a device first created for the convenience of a portable telephone. About a third of the congregation does not own one of these devices. And yet Todd who is of the tech-savvy generation finds company and meaning among this group of people. He worships with them. He studies with them, following the text on his smartphone screen. He participates in the work of ordering the life of the congregation, providing Google search answers in the meetings.

If I were trying to create a new harmonious group, I would not invite Todd. Or I would not invite the other ninety, sixty, or thirty like the ones presently in my congregation and instead invite only a lot of Todds. Lucky for me and us the Spirit operates by a different logic.

Every congregation has dissonance in the composition of its membership, people who do not fit together in an easy or natural way. Sometimes people talk about small churches as family chapels as if the presence of a dominant family cancels out the friction of diverse personalities. Those who grew up in large extended families know that is not true. But even so, every congregation also has the Spirit's presence and pressure.

Before "unity in a diversity" in the church is a human aspiration, it is a divine action. Paul does not say we should try to create a synergy of body and parts (1 Cor 12); that is happening already. The Spirit creates and sustains community. Our role is to recognize the Spirit's work, cooperate with it, and invite new persons into its field of force.

The Spirit Makes God Present in the Worship

The Spirit visits a people whose vitality is as spent as a valley of sun-bleached bones and resuscitates (Ezek 37). The Spirit descends on persons who do not speak the same language and creates a new community through the miracle of a commonly received message about the fate of one Jesus of Nazareth (Acts 2). The Spirit coaxes persons with monotheistic loyalties gathered in house churches into a novel worship of Lord Jesus that includes confessing the name (1 Cor 12:3), singing his praises (Eph 5:19), and praying to him (1 Cor 1:2). This Spirit who visits, descends, and coaxes is present in the gathered worship of God's people today without regard for numbers present (Matt 18:20).

The good preachers I know pretend otherwise. They act as though the weight of the worship service is upon them. They accrue disciplines of rhetoric. They study the texts of the church and the contexts in which they minister. They prepare well and have butterflies in the stomach as they get up to preach. When they connect with the people all is right with the world. God is present and God has smiled. When they fail to connect they are miserable and look for some clergy equivalent of a baseball batter who strikes out and throws his bat in disgust. God was not smiling and perhaps was not even present.

But this is a game of pretend, and those same good preachers know when to quit playing. They value the times of being borne in worship: the respite from the heightened self-consciousness of leadership during music, the unscripted wisdom of an eight-year-old during the children's message, the impact of a sermon that far surpasses the preacher's expectations. It is as if there is a prior power and presence.

At all times but especially in the preacher's seasons of self-doubt and in those times of doubting the viability of the congregation, egocentric illusions must give way to the reality of the Spirit's work in making God present in worship. Before the posture of flexing for maximum impact, there is the posture of leaning on something greater than one's self. Before the question "What must I do?" there is the question "What is the direction of the flow in which I find myself?"

The Spirit Gives to the Congregation Every Spiritual Gift It Needs

Paul writes to a house church, likely thirty to forty persons. He tells this small group that by the grace of God given them in Jesus Christ they have been enriched by spiritual gifts. They have been enriched not selectively, not sparingly, but "in everything" (1 Cor 1:5). Paul counts those ways later in the same letter and elsewhere. There are spiritual gifts that build up the body, like service, teaching, and exhortation. There are spiritual gifts that equip the body for ministry and mission, including faith, healing, and giving. And there are spiritual gifts that provide release, reform, and renewal, such as discernment, speaking in tongues, and prophecy.[7]

You have everything you need, Paul tells the small church at Corinth: "…you aren't missing any spiritual gift while you wait for our Lord Jesus Christ" (1 Cor 1:7). It is a word of hope for all congregations. It is a remarkable word of hope for small congregations. Their size is not indicative of their potential. Behind the seasons of scarcity there is an original plentitude. Beneath the surface of unimpressive and settled institutional life, the fire of the Spirit's gifts waits to break through and break out.

I preached a series about spiritual gifts to a congregation that averaged twenty-seven persons in worship. One of those persons was Helen. Helen's work was as a high school custodian, and her joy was her family. But her personal obsession was "the Lord's tongue." For several years she had been working to teach herself Hebrew using an old grammar and an interlinear Hebrew Old Testament that she picked up at a church garage sale. As one who was nearly drummed out of graduate school for failing to clear the hurdle of Hebrew, I could appreciate the degree of difficulty of Helen's accomplishment: the writing backward, the mastering of jots and tittles, the absence of an environment where it could be heard spoken.

Helen had been using what we both agreed could be called "a gift of tongues" in her prayer life and to adorn scripture passages on Christmas cards. After the sermon series we began to explore other avenues for using that gift to build up the body, such as reading the Old Testament in "the Lord's tongue" in worship. The

Sunday Helen read Exodus 3 in Hebrew and English—the call of Moses with the giving of the divine name, "I am who I am" —was a high and holy moment in the worshipping life of the congregation.

The Spirit Seeks to Reform and Revive the Congregation

God's spirit moves like a wind over an unfinished creation (Gen 1:2) and *separates* (Gen 1:4, 7); *gathers* (Gen 1:9); *commands fruitfulness* (Gen 1:11-12, 22); *aligns systems* (Gen 1:14-18); and *diversifies* (Gen 1:21-22, 24-25). All this occurs before God introduces the first humans into creation to "till it and keep it" (Gen 2:15).

God's spirit moves like a wind over the unfinished congregation and separates, gathers, commands fruitfulness, aligns systems, diversifies, and does whatever else is needed to reform and revive that congregation. We usually talk about this work in terms of large historical movements associated with intriguing leaders. There was the protestant reformation led by Luther, Calvin, and Zwingli. There was the Great Awakening led by George Whitefield, John Wesley, and Jonathan Edwards. Sometimes the Spirit called the church at large to recover some neglected element of its core identity such as the singular call (monasticism), the accountability of small groups (Pietism), or a prophetic word against idolatry (the confessing church in Nazi Germany). Sometimes the Spirit breathed new life into what appeared to be a hopeless valley of dry bones: the Second Great Awakening, the Azusa Street Revival, or the post-World War II revival.

Two things to remember: first, there is always a "people's history" to be told about these movements of reform and revival, the part played by the common persons in the pews who received and cooperated with the Spirit's impulses. And second, the Spirit's gifts, including the impulses toward reform and revival, are promised not just to the church at large but to all congregations of every size.

Sometimes even here, in this small congregation, in this small corner of creation, the Spirit *separates* (e.g., inspires a change in leadership), *gathers* (e.g., reveals a new target constituency), *commands fruitfulness* (e.g., gives one of us an inner call that leads to a new ministry), *aligns systems* (e.g., surfaces a corporate vision), and *diversifies* (e.g., moves us to receive the unscripted contributions of the younger generations). In the words of the psalmist, "This has happened because of the LORD; it is astounding in our sight!" (Ps 118:23).

Memory Restored

The exercise in selective amnesia is ended. The weight of bearing criticisms, critiques, and caricatures returns. This is part of the "professional knowledge" of the pastor of a small church, the insider stuff that populates that pastor's workday stream of consciousness with nagging questions. Do we have enough resources to be "church"? Can this congregation be saved, or is the decline irreversible? Is serving *here* what God had in mind in calling me to ministry?

From time to time it may be helpful for the pastor to imagine life without the censoring of such "professional knowledge." Think, for example, of the technical term *mainline decline*. As professional shoptalk goes, it is a relatively recent technical term that rose to prominence in the late 1960s and early '70s and was taught to pastors in their professional and trade schools.

Most in the congregation may be vaguely aware that the gathered congregation is not what it used to be. Some may remember "better days" of community influence, nuclear families, and financial stability. But they do not labor under the pastor's institutional perspective or the specialist education that included courses in sociology of religion. They do not worship, minister, make decisions, and witness in the community through the fog of a constant suspicion of mainline decline. And therefore, they may see signs of vitality missed by the pastor.

For the pastor there is no going back to a precritical experience of the congregation; but there may be a going forward to a second naiveté. We will argue for the power of direct observation and theological reflection to uncover the native vitality of small congregations in the areas of worship, soul care, order, and community witness. The pastor can bend in close and observe. The pastor can project into the humble congregation of ninety, sixty, or thirty the church's grand language about God and the church in the hopeful search of resonance.

Chapter 2

MAINTAINING WORSHIP

Every Sunday morning between 10:00 and 10:15 about eighty to ninety persons gather in the sanctuary at 700 Market Street, Lemoyne, Pennsylvania, to maintain worship as others before them have done for a hundred years. They do this "in season and out of season." They do it in spite of the impact of large public events like changes in the economy, wars, and the advent of social media. They do it in spite of failures in pastoral leadership. They were maintaining worship before I came as their pastor, and they will be doing it after I am gone.

This is the basic undeniable, intractable, and inescapable fact about life in a small church. These ninety, sixty, or thirty people will assemble week after week for a sixty-minute worship service. They will honor God with their praise and worship; they will attend to the reading and unfolding of God's word; they will be cleansed and energized by the sacraments; they will renew ties that bind them to others there; they will bring offerings to the Lord; and then they will scatter, only to repeat the same six days and twenty-three hours later.

As a pastor I am humbled in the presence of this phenomenon. The fifteen minutes before it starts have become some of the most important of my week. I sit up front near the lectern and watch them trickle in: the arthritic ninety-something veterans who take their Aleve, grab their walkers, and grit their way into the sanctuary, collapsing into their favorite seats; the young families who enter like the multi-headed hydra of Greek mythology, talking to and past one another, enveloping then moving past greeters and ushers as they make their way down the aisle and try to settle in a single pew; the shy, bookish homeless man who washed up in the men's room and changed into his respectful Sunday shoes, white shirt, and necktie, then settled into his space along an aisle where he is approachable by others. This day, church will happen again.

As a pastor caught up in the currents of larger church anxiety, I must confess I have not always been so kind in my assessment of the assembled congregation. I have coddled them as if they were passive spectators needing to be entertained. I have reduced worship to an educational experience as if they were primarily students who want nothing more than to take home a few good facts. At times I have even scolded them for *being there* instead of being elsewhere in a more activist or extroverted posture!

Lately I prefer to look first for "the soul of the congregation" in worship.[1] At a minimum it is a living culture in its most conspicuous expression. There are *artifacts* like the stained glass window above the altar showing Jesus praying in Gethsemane. There are *practices* like the eight-year-old acolyte Leo reverencing the altar as he learned from the fourteen-year-old acolyte Gabby. There are *values* such as anticipating the Lord's Meal on the first Sunday of the month. There are *signals of meaning* like the deference shown noisy children. There are *views of the world* such as "us praying for them." This assembled congregation is a "thick text" worthy of a careful read.

And it is a "thick text" infused with the Spirit who seeks to make God feel present to all by descending and moving over the congregation. In the verbs of the church's poets, the Spirit weans from lesser things, lifts dimness of soul, quiets doubt and rebellion, focuses and intensifies love for God.[2] The Spirit reveals the things of God, personalizes God's saving work, and inspires faith that moves mountains.[3] The Spirit alternately harnesses emotions in singing and praying or sets them free for moaning and shouting.[4] The Spirit gives "new eyes for seeing, new hands for holding on" to those in the congregation with whom the journey of faith is shared.[5]

I must cooperate with that Spirit. I must play my assigned role in that vital culture. I am present to *conduct* worship, not only as in managing or supervising, but also as in coordinating and orchestrating the energy and the elements that are already there.

Clues to Local Religious Creativity

I will look for clues as to what should/could/may be there in the worshipping congregation wherever I can find them. In recent years two clues in particular have captured my imagination and expanded my thinking. The first came from my reading of hundreds of local church versions of their founding story. In dozens of workshops that I conducted, I asked the lay and clergy leaders of small churches to retrieve the story of their congregation's beginnings either in surviving documents or in the best available oral tradition.

Up to that time, I operated with a Johnny Appleseed explanation for the startup of new churches. A well-equipped solitary figure heroically carried the gospel to a secular location, planted

25

the precious seed, and soon the crop of a congregation sprang up. That figure was an itinerant preacher on horseback. The implication was clear: if the Conference, Synod, Presbytery, Classis, or Association did not send out that pioneer planter, the church at large would have remained an East Coast urban movement.

The founding stories I received told a different story. They told of laypersons gathering in homes, offices, schools, stores, and under arbors for worship, which at a minimum included group praying, singing, and attention to the scriptures. The visits of a traveling preacher certainly mattered. When he arrived he would preside over baptisms, weddings, and memorial services. He would consolidate the order of the young movement of believers: naming and blessing of leaders; distributing tracts, Bibles, and hymnals; setting the time for the next visit. The itinerant preacher connected the local congregation to the larger connection of churches, but the fire was there before he arrived and it would be sustained locally for years, sometimes decades, before a settled pastor could become a regular presence in that congregation.[6]

The second clue to local religious creativity came from a study of worship in the first house churches of the New Testament. It is estimated that the largest room for worship at this time allowed only about twenty-five to forty persons. When Acts reports "the Lord added daily to the community…" (2:47), it is not saying a central congregation was becoming bigger; it is saying these house churches were proliferating. But what was the worship like in these house churches? What was the source of its energy and loyalty?

I answered with something like a "great person theory of leadership," that is, changes in history are to be explained by certain persons with an unusual measure of the traits of leadership such as energy, intelligence, ability to communicate, and endurance. The great person I had in mind was of course the Apostle Paul, and the relation that I projected him as having to the churches to whom he wrote his letters was that of a theologian and teacher. The role I assigned to the persons in those churches was something like a passive group of students, though sometimes given to misbehaving in class. So follow Paul's development as a theologian (for example, his use of concepts of divinity borrowed from the Greek worldview to speak to Gentile Christians), and you understand what's happening in the New Testament worship.

What I have come to appreciate lately is the emerging picture of a flowering of local religious creativity in those first-century churches, a dynamic movement in which Paul participated and contributed but did not invent. It was, in the words of one of the New Testament scholars who helped to name this movement, "a virtual explosion of devotion to Jesus." In local house churches, in diverse settings, and with only minimal support from a connection of churches beyond, there is a widespread outbreak of worship practices where Jesus is the focus of worship and local creativity in the service of that worship is evident.[7]

The persons gathered in these house churches worship and pray to the Lord Jesus (Acts 7:59-60; 13:2; 1 Cor 16:21-24; 2 Cor 12:8-9; Rev 22:20)—a remarkable feat in itself considering most of them are fiercely monotheistic.[8] They receive and share prophetic messages from Jesus (Act 18:9-10; 1 Cor 12:4-11; Rev 2–3) and improvise interpretations of texts from the Hebrew scriptures to include Jesus (Acts 2:17-21/Joel 2:28-32; Acts 5:30/Deut 21:22-23). They practice confessing "Jesus is Lord!" knowing the risks of such a confession when they return to the public square (Rom 10:9-13; 1 Cor 12:3; Phil 2:10-11). They playfully intertwine "God" and "Jesus" in prayers and blessings (Rom 1:8; 1 Thess 3:11-13; 2 Thess 2:16-17; 3:5). They sing psalms, hymns, and spiritual songs to Jesus (Col 3:16-17; Eph 5:18-20; Phil 2:6-11).⁹

The Search for Local Religious Creativity

I gather such clues where I can, and I summon them in the service of being a better pastor of a small church, especially at the point of worship. I bring to that worship the tools with which my theological education has equipped me: clues that there might be something more there than first impressions allow; a repertoire of language for naming the raw data I encounter; and a simple beginning premise that the church is a creation of the Spirit. And so armed, I search for what might be there.

Their Singing Voice

They gather and sing. The local church is one of the few remaining places where people do that in contemporary American society. They sing about a third of the worship hour: hymns, doxology, benediction, with the occasional Malotte's "The Lord's Prayer" and sung responses during the Lord's Meal. For another ten to fifteen minutes, they listen to others sing or play music.

They resonate to certain tunes or genres more than others. They have their favorite hymns. Calvary's anthem is the Shaker-inspired "Lord of the Dance,"¹⁰ though no one can explain why. Since the song was introduced in a 1989 hymnal, the congregation has shown a preference for it in worship, weddings, and hymn sings. So I will look to this hymn for hints to the religious character of this congregation.

Their Jesus is confident and determined in his mission. He dances in his heavenly preexistence before coming to dance on the earth. He dances equally before fishermen who will follow and the scribe and Pharisee who will not. Their Jesus will expose and provoke the undeniable forces of fear and destruction in this world: "it's hard to dance with a devil on your back."[11] The imagery resonates with tender spots in the corporate memory. But their Jesus will have the last word ("they cut me down and I leapt up high"[12]), and his final victory motivates and reflects their gritty determination. The lead metaphor, "dance," hints at a receptivity to a greater use of the arts in worship.

I will look to the congregation's signature hymns. What do they tell me about their corporate character, their theological inclinations, their participation in larger public events? What congregational assets do they suggest? What symptoms of arrested theological development should I pick up on and then address as the resident theologian?

For most of their past small churches were filled with the sound of harmonious singing, the blending of four distinct voices. Those old enough to have experienced such singing in worship know it is hard to imagine a more potent metaphor of the church as one body with several members working together (1 Cor 12:12-26). The highest soprano or tenor, the lowest base, the person in the alto middle, each makes a contribution, and the whole is more than the sum of its individual parts.

Four-part harmony in church has deteriorated over the last few decades. Some say it was the loss of the organ accompaniment, others the dropping of the choral amen; many cite the projection of lyrics only onto the screen replacing the use of hymnals. The loss of a culture of choral music outside the church certainly played a part. On the positive side, a variety of musical forms have been introduced into worship, forms that do not require the four-part harmonizing, such as black gospel, praise and worship, Latin American coritos, and Taizé.

This is generally good news for small churches where the lead instrument is likely to be a piano, keyboard, or guitar and drums. But I would argue for the deliberate attempt to sustain a culture of four-part harmony singing in small churches as a compelling mark of their uniqueness. Small congregations are best positioned to imitate and become robust choirs. Visitors should experience the disciplined harmonizing, the majesty of individuals singing robustly in the service of a haunting larger product, the corporate melodious praise of God. Visitors should leave with earworms from that encounter.

So as the final leader of worship I will cherish the residual pieces of the congregation's four-part harmony singing and in concert with our musicians seek to build on them. Perhaps we should introduce singing practice into the worship or at other congregational gatherings. Perhaps we should develop a signature a cappella verse to be used in the weekly worship. Perhaps we should borrow from other traditions of congregational harmonizing. At Calvary, we are experimenting with the Moravian practice of *Singstunde* where on an occasional Sunday we will sing a string of hymn verses in place of the sermon. The verses are lifted from various hymns and strung together according to theological themes, doctrines, or arguments.

Intercessory prayer

Their Prayer Voice

After serving for twenty years in larger churches and in specialized ministries, I returned to a small church. My first experience of culture shock came in the worship service at the point of the intercessions. The list was long. The language was blunt. The emotional investment was raw.

In a larger church setting it is simply impossible to allow such a phenomenon. It would interrupt the flow of worship. It would turn worship into a prayer meeting. Individual intercessions must be edited and channeled. Specificity must give way to the generic.

Given my larger church instincts I was at first uncomfortable, even a little embarrassed by the small church's practice of intercessions. Whether spoken by them in the service or passed to me on scraps of paper to be read outload, I found myself resisting. Too personal! Too commonplace! Too close to violating HIPAA laws!

The prayers for health specified concrete victories in the larger warfare of MS or heart disease. The prayers for family members might be as big as financial recovery from bankruptcy and as small as finding a lost hunting license. At Calvary, we have a hands-on ministry with people living on the margin of society. That has added a whole other layer of desperate needs. People hand in their requests on scraps of paper to the kitchen volunteers or leave cards at the prayer box at the main entrance to the sanctuary. Their heart-felt requests conjure up images of being one paycheck away from eviction, living in a car that may not pass inspection, or being mugged while one slept in the park on a summer's night. "Please pray for me!"

Eventually my discomfort with the prayer voice of the small church gave way to curiosity, and curiosity gave way to respect. There was something primitive and authentic going on here, an energy not available in larger worship settings. I began to look for ways to name it, not for their sake (they take it for granted) but for mine. And I found myself coming back to the prayer vocals of the Bible.

In the Bible prayer is alternately deeply personal and deeply communal. One moment it is the individual cutting through the fog of everyday interference to touch the divine: *Help, Thanks, Wow,* as Anne Lamott so nicely summarizes.[13] And the next moment prayer is the community of faith addressing God in praise, complaint, petition, lament, or thanksgiving with the magnified intensity of a corporate voice.

We may think of these two prayer voices as comfortably discrete. Lots of people seem to pray fine without going to church. Lots of churchgoers seem to get along with a minimum of prayer during the week. But in the Bible, especially highlighted in the Psalms, the vitality of the individual's prayer life is very closely tied to participation in the prayer practices of the community of faith. The individual at prayer is a reflection of the congregation at prayer; the "I" of the prayer is never far from the "we" of the assembled people of God. In some passages of the Bible the two voices spill over into one another. In Psalm 44, for instance, the psalmist alternately prays, "*We* have heard it, God, with *our* own ears" (v. 1) and "You who are *my* king," (v. 4) and then "I won't trust in *my* bow" (v. 6) followed by "So *we* glory in God at all times" (v. 8).

Now I get what my place is. I am there to help at the intersection of the two prayer voices in the congregation, to receive, preserve, and share publicly the raw intercessions of individual souls. I may edit gently here and there, but not so much that

I/we can no longer hear the pain of desperate persons calling upon the Lord.

At the same time, I am there to build up the prayer voice of the congregation at large, to supply the better language for our shared vocals of praise, complaints, petitions, laments, and thanksgivings. So I will borrow the language of the psalms to bolster a "we" that encompasses but transcends the individual dramas. We will pray together the poetry of our hymns and the masterpieces from the books of prayer so that we may sustain a high level of God-awareness and an awareness of spiritual connection with believers across time. And I will share the most relevant and timely prayers from the cornucopia of contemporary prayers accessible online from churches across local and distant cultures to keep our praying fresh, pointed, and spirited.

Their Call Response

Neither I nor the small churches where I have preached through the years were prepared for an engaging exchange! There was no black church or Pentecostal tradition of the preacher buoyed up by the constant and sometimes witty retorts from the congregation. They were not practiced in call and response singing even though their hymnals contained such pieces. They could usually remember the name of the last Amen Charlie; they just couldn't imagine how he would fit into the present worship.

I wasn't much better prepared. In seminary the emphasis was on preaching as the delivery of theological truth. We accrued the tools for research: Hebrew and Greek, word studies and commentaries, theology books and, to guarantee contemporary relevance, newspapers. We were given sequential steps for moving from the first translation to the finished manuscript and told it would take about twenty hours to get there if you did it right. Delivering that manuscript to the congregation was an afterthought.

It was a formula for disappointment. I would read at them, occasionally looking up for some hint of recognition in their faces. They would listen or pretend to listen quietly. We would both breathe a sigh of relief when it was over. The situation is improved today with the renewed interest in the art of rhetoric. There are best practices for arranging one's material, projecting one's voice, expressing with one's hands and eyes that yield a stronger resonance with the congregation.[14]

But rhetoric is dealing with only one side of the equation. How can the congregation become more mentally and emotionally engaged in the sermon? There are opportunities available in the small-church setting that are not available in larger settings, such as the potential for a more intimate preaching connection. The faces of the ninety, sixty, or thirty are familiar to the preacher. The preacher carries the outlines if not the intricacies of their stories as a body of knowledge. And the preacher can summon this body of knowledge to elicit a livelier response to the call of the message.

In a sermon series comparing the gospel and the game of baseball, I was pleased to discover and then incorporate into the messages a retired umpire, a relative of one of the Rockford Peaches (the women's baseball team depicted in the movie *A League of Their Own*), and the landlord who rented to minor league players on their way to the majors. They were all regular-attending members.

It took a little digging to bring out the compelling details. Then more time was needed to weave their anecdotes into the text of the sermon and their artifacts into accompanying PowerPoint slides. But time taken away from what? As you become seasoned in ministry you realize that the exegetical consensus on the texts you are most likely to preach does not change overnight. It changes— and you must keep up—but more likely over years and even decades. Once you pay the rent of absorbing the current exegetical consensus, where can you go? You can try for clever and eccentric interpretations, but they detract from the straightforward power of "plain truth for plain people,"[15] and that power is needed today more than ever.

So why not invest more time in building up the congregation's capacity to project themselves into the message? A sermon series on the great birth narratives of the Bible can be the occasion to gather and share baby pictures. Another series on the "fear not" pronouncements of the Bible can explore their favorite experiences with the horror genre in film. The goal is to discover the points of contact that make the sermon more like a call and response and less like a soliloquy. The scale of the small church allows for broad participation.

Their Penchant for Color

The vitality of a small congregation can be measured aesthetically. It is not a foolproof metric. There are, for example, vibrant small faith communities meeting in drab environments for the sake of missionary presence and others marking time until they can occupy a building they intend to beautify to the glory of God. But most small churches occupy a space that is under their control, a space that they can transform into a "thin space" through the mediums of beauty—or not!

I have seen small congregations where the dispirited condition registers in their neglect of visual aesthetics. They are immune to the eyesores that scream at first-time visitors. They tolerate symbols that send unintended messages. They accept fatalistically an earlier generation's taste in art. They settle into a worship environment of faded colors and forgotten visual paths as if they were disincarnated souls expecting to meet God in some "left behind" scenario.

No doubt the leader's role in those situations is to deal first with the specific causes of the dispirited condition, though I have seen a "dress for success" approach work too. That is, by attending early to the visuals a foothold is gained for the long work of restoring the congregation's health—a bouquet of flowers for the patient.

In most small churches, among the gathered congregation, there is still a native penchant for color in worship, a local appetite for and gravitation toward visual beauty. Not to Moses the leader or to Aaron the priest, but to Bezalel and Oholiab, workers with their hands, does the Spirit give "skill, ability, and knowledge" to bring the added value of beauty to the holiness of the tabernacle (Exod 31:1-11). My role as leader is to cooperate with that penchant, to let it flourish with a gentle push here or pull there.

The colors of the church's seasons are a good place to start. We conduct our congregational worship against the story of Jesus as told in blue, gold and white, purple, black, gold and white again, red, and green (or some such variation). I have found it fruitful to amplify the connection. Replace worn or dated altar, lectern, and pulpit covers. Recruit acolytes from among the children and clothe them in the seasonal vestments purchased or hand sewn. Vested acolytes, like vested clergy, reinforce the corporate drama that worship is even in a small setting. Adorned in the colors of the meta story of Jesus, they remind all present of the true home of individual stories.

The front of the sanctuary is another blank canvas worthy of attention. There will be those spaces marked as special by sparsity, the table that holds the elements for communion, for instance. But there are floor spaces, wall spaces, abandoned furniture from an earlier generation's taste for the holy, assorted nooks and crannies, all available to the local religious creativity of the congregation.

Giving expression to the seasons of the church is an obvious place to start. Working in fabrics, flowers, symbols, packaged groceries, books, lighting, color schemes, wood and metal, and hooks and wires, the Bezalels and Oholiabs of the congregation create an arresting visual focus for the worship: the images of expectation in Advent, the images of betrayal and violence in Lent, the images of the descending Spirit in Pentecost.

Then there are the seasons of the nature that can be captured in small plants, flowers, leaves, harvest fruits, canned goods, gardening instruments, antiques and artifacts from house, garage, or barn, toys, seasonal sports equipment, stuffed or ceramic birds, fish, insects, and animals set against a background of the many shades of red, yellow, blue, and their combinations played out in the course of the annual cycle. A sermon series may suggest a layer of visuals on top of these displays: baseball hats, NASCAR models, framed pictures, medical equipment, musical instruments.

As the pastoral leader the point I want to remember is that even in this small congregation there is a native energy for visual creativity that can be tapped in the common service of worshipping God. It is not confined to one or two "artistic types," though they may have to produce the pilot displays and model the boundaries between taste and kitsch.[16] It is an enterprise for the congregation at large: to take the canvas it has been given— stained glass or clear glass windows, oversized or rightsized space, clear architectural messages or mixed architectural messages— and, "filled...with the divine spirit" (Exod 31:3), transform it so that the people of God may experience a more complete and lasting worship of God.

Their Witness

The suspense that hangs in the air of every congregation on Sunday morning is the suspense of King Zedekiah's anxious question to the prophet Jeremiah, "Is there a word from the LORD?" (Jer 37:17). We the gathered people pause to ask and to wait. Will the ruler of the universe who has instructed us to "call upon the name of the Lord" speak? Will the one who is so good at interrupting our frivolous, distorted, obsessed interior monologues, interrupt them one more time with a divine "fear not," "peace," or simply, "cool it!"? The character of God, if not the very existence of God, could be called into question by God's perceived silence. Elijah's mockery of the prophets of the false god Baal could be turned against us by others or even by ourselves. "Shout louder! Certainly he's a god! Perhaps he is lost in thought or wandering or traveling somewhere. Or maybe he is asleep and must wake up!" (1 Kgs 18:27).

"Is there a word from the Lord?" Resolution of the suspense comes when Jeremiah reports, "There is!" And our first assumption is that the one called by God and authorized by the community will bring that word from God: the preacher. It is a fair assumption but it is incomplete. As the preacher I am especially equipped and sent by the community of faith to search for a word from the Lord and report back. But as a believer among believers I am as much Zedekiah as I am Jeremiah. I, too, need to know whether God is really out there and engaged in the life of the members of the worshipping congregations. Next to the sermon, the witness from the persons in the pews is the most important venue for receiving a word from the Lord.

In 2008 my denomination began to include the promise to witness to the established list of four vows of church membership: to uphold the church with one's prayers, presence, gifts, and service. It was not so much the introduction of a new thing as it was the reconnection with a lost part of our religious heritage.[17] Other denominations were making similar reconnections with their traditions of "witness" or "testimony."

It can be helpful to designate a space for "witness" in the weekly bulletin whether there will be one or not. The very name carries its own nervous energy. It provokes associations of religious bragging, uncontrolled emotions, and poor public speaking. But in time these can be replaced with associations of authentic speech, necessary release of emotions, and, so crucial for an appreciation of the small church setting, the localness of religious experience. In this very congregation, among these very ordinary-looking people—not many wise, not many powerful, not many of upper class, says Paul (1 Cor 1:26)—the same God directing the stars in their courses and intervening for good in large public events is at work with the simple expectation that those who receive grace should talk about it. "Cry out to me whenever you are in trouble; I will deliver you, then you will honor me" (Ps 50:15).

I am the behind-the-scenes coach. I encourage developing witnesses, offer pointers in public speaking, set the boundaries, and guarantee the venue. When needed, I introduce. Afterward, I

39

help witnesses receive the responses they have generated, while at the same time keeping myself and the service open to that occasional spontaneous witness, knowing that "real" counts for more than "polished."

Most of the witnesses offered will be in the genre of *providence*. Persons who have just passed through some transition or have experienced a triumphant anniversary will talk about detours taken and course corrections made, about signs and wonders along the way: the soldier home from assignment, the college graduate, the survivor of a car wreck, the recently employed after a season of unemployment, the couple celebrating their sixty-fifth wedding anniversary.

The *healing* witness takes the congregation into the chaos of a life story interrupted by a severe diagnosis or other traumatic health event. There may be frank words of righteous anger as there are in the psalms, but they give way to other reports from the front: the miraculous touch, the discovery of healing given in one place while denied in another, the slow but sure work of reconstructing a new life narrative with a greater place for God in it.

I give the name *biblical echo* to a genre of witness where persons have gone through an intense experience that ignites in them a strong affinity with certain biblical characters, images, words, stories, or parables. It is as if they have been enlisted from above to personify some facet of the scriptures. The recent victim of corporate downsizing finds wisdom in the resilient manager of Jesus's parable (Luke 16). The woman who miraculously reconnects with a long-lost relative finds words for the intensity of the first face-to-face meeting in the reunion of Jacob and Esau (Gen 33). The one whose journey to faith began in angry resistance but ends in surrender and new purpose finds resonance in Paul's conversion on the road to Damascus (Acts 9).

And I give the name *hello goodbye* to the several witnesses I have coaxed from persons new to the faith community or getting ready to leave. Both types are in a unique position to hold up a mirror to the congregation. Those joining can report the practices of hospitality that drew them in, but also any first impressions that had to be overcome. They can tell why they prefer this congregation to larger ones. And those leaving can thank the congregation for the gifts given them for their journey. A special class of persons in this group are the young adults who are present for a season while attending school, stationed at a base, or apprenticing in their jobs. We don't hold them, but we are energized by their visit.

Maintaining with Excellence

Before "maintenance" was a disease to be cured or bad habit to be broken, it was a virtue to be learned and practiced. It is most akin to the classical virtue of courage, a capacity to overcome fear and hold steady in the face of threat. There is something heroic about the old language of maintenance applied to worship. The founding document of my denomination talks about the church's existence "for the edification of believers" and "the redemption of the world." But before both, the church, "under the discipline of the Holy Spirit," exists "to provide for the maintenance of worship."[18]

If you allow it, the phrase conjures up images of drama. A house church gathers discretely in a country where Christians are persecuted. A prayer group takes their corporate story up a _maintaining church_

Chapter 2

notch to the discipline of a weekly public service. A new church start announces a time and place, puts out the welcome mat, and holds the first worship service, followed by another and another and another regardless of the fluctuating numbers. A congregation that loses its building to a fire gathers the very next Sunday in the borrowed space of another congregation or in a school and repeats the familiar order of worship. Christians who were once a majority but now are "resident aliens" conspicuously assemble to honor God on Sunday morning when most others don't.

I want to include the small church in that list. It maintains worship week after week, "in season and out of season." Its numbers grow but do not grow in quantum leaps. Its numbers fluctuate but there is always a solid core. And these faithful waste no energy envying larger gatherings, wishing they could be something they are not. As best they can for as long as they can, they will gather weekly to worship the Lord "in Spirit and truth" (John 4:24). "In Spirit": animated by the Spirit's presence that is evident not only in the gifts of the trained pastoral leader but also and especially in the local religious creativity of the people.

And "in truth" because those who lead the worship, from pastor to musicians, from ushers to acolytes sustain a culture of review and perfection. The intimacy and the informality of worship in the small church may be the prevailing climate, but within that climate the elements of worship (its prayers, music, visuals, sacraments) and the execution of worship (its singing, preaching, movements, pageantry) are the subject of a constant, non-defensive conversation initiated by leaders.

Those leaders know what is at stake: worship is the most important thing small churches do together. The leaders saw what they saw and heard what they heard: the paraments are frayed and

42

discolored with age, the congregation is dawdling on the hymns, the print on the screen is too small, the sound system crackles and pops, guests are left to fend for themselves, the organ is wheezing. They don't dismiss these signals, but report them and agitate for their correction. They know they are not exempt from the call to excellence in worship by virtue of the size of the gathered congregation. They know that the capacity to care about and address flaws is a measure of their corporate will to live.

Chapter 3

SOUL CARE

They do not come to worship hoping to be swept up into the gravity of my agenda, these ninety, sixty, or thirty souls. They are not there to hear me wax eloquent about the things that consume me as a called and equipped pastor: the continued disestablishment of the church, the mainline decline, the bishop's appeal for disaster relief, the needed repairs on the roof, the annual meeting, the loss of biblical literacy, the larger social questions that won't go away, the connectional church's debate on sexuality, a postcolonial reading of the Bible, the increase of our impact for good in the community, and so on. Much of leadership is taking people where they would not go on their own. Growing up in Christ means enlarging your horizon of care. But these are destinations not starting lines. I must meet them at their starting lines.

They begin at *life*! They begin at the things that consume their weekday hours and keep them awake at night. One of them graduated from college a year ago, four years of hard work behind her, a big debt in front of her, and she still hasn't been able to find a job in her field. Another one has just been told by his doctor that they are down to the last experimental protocol to address his aggressive cancer. Still another wonders what other loss of powers will accompany her MS and how soon. And so on and on for the ninety, sixty, or thirty faces of the weekly congregation and maybe a dozen more who are homebound.

The tradition of the care of souls in the community of faith is deeply biblical. It is justified by the worth of each person created in the image and likeness of God (Gen 1:26) and the worth of their specific journey through the stages of life (Ps 71). It is affirmed by the God-questions that arise from sudden reversals of fortune (Job), from moral failure (Ps 51), from natural disasters (Ps 121), from experiences of shame (Ps 31) and experiences of dislocation (Ps 22). And most of all, it is validated by the healing ministry of Jesus, by the conspicuous fact that Jesus spends so much of the short time of his public ministry laying hands on persons to pray for their healing.

Soul Care and Church Size

All pastors are called to the care of souls. They share with their colleagues in the medical field a primary vow of nonmaleficence, a promise to do no harm to vulnerable persons under their care. They extend the healing benefits of God in many ways, but especially by their timely visits and genuine prayers. They lead ministries that address the well-being of the whole person. They look for the beneficial intersection of the stories of the individual, of the community of faith, and of the Bible. They distribute the healing benefits of the Lord's Meal.

All pastors are more or less equipped for the care of souls. They take required courses in pastoral care and counseling. Some do advanced work in clinical pastoral education (CPE). They learn current theories and best practices. They experiment with models of soul care that variously emphasize the place of such factors as cultural context, lay participation, or short-term opportunities. They begin the lifelong work of trying out conversation partners for their soul care, now the twentieth-century psychologists with their personality theories, now pastoral theologians who mine the biblical texts for their original wisdom, now the fathers and mothers of the ancient church who first explored the terrain of the Christian soul and left markers.

All pastors are called to the care of souls, not some in certain settings. About forty years ago a pioneering study commissioned for the Episcopal Church, *Sizing Up a Congregation for New Member Ministry*,[1] analyzed the distinctiveness of the cultures of congregations by their size. Arlin Rothauge labeled churches according to their active membership as *family church* (0-50), *pastoral church* (50-150), *program church* (150-350), and *corporation church* (350-500+). The Rothauge analysis and labeling of congregational cultures has had widespread acceptance. It has proved helpful in a number of ways, but especially at the point of its intended purpose, which was to identify the distinctive ways new members are drawn to, assimilated into, and held by congregations of various sizes.

There are pastoral implications in Rothauge's analysis, and at this point it is less helpful. In fact, that analysis has helped to perpetuate harmful stereotypes of both the small church and the vocation of soul care. According to Rothauge, the relevant location for the pastor's exercise of soul care is in the two smaller sizes of congregations. In the *family church* (0-50) pastors have "a special kind of contact" that allows them to offer "regular friendship," and to act as "a spiritual guide and confessor." In the *pastoral church*

(50-150) that soul care is stretched but still has primary impact. In so far as the pastor can extend spiritual friendships to the larger number of persons it generates loyalty to the pastor and thereby to the congregation. But how many spiritually caring relationships can one pastor have? The pastor must learn "the necessity of moving on to others."

In the *program church* (150-350) the pastor, now called "leader," cannot maintain pastoral contact with the whole congregation, but instead must delegate that role to others. The congregation must make the transition from "dependency" on that leader for "basic ministry functions" including counseling and spiritual growth. The pastor of persons must become the facilitator of processes. And in the *corporation church* (350-500+) that leader must steward the congregation's sense of purpose and provide executive leadership at a distance for its caring ministries while specialists provide soul care within and beyond the congregation. Persons in the congregation may have a strong identification with the lead pastor, to the point of "legendary status," but that pastor would not be expected to provide individual soul care.[2]

The call to care for souls transcends the context for ministry. There is no running from it into distant executive positions of preaching or administration. Some introverted pastors may daydream of the day when they can assign that care to staff. Some ambitious pastors may assume that a passion for the vitality of the corporate congregation is enough; "I don't do hospital!" as one such person put it. But most pastors, in all settings, practice some soul care because they know that is where real life is happening for their parishioners and because it is an intractable element of their call. Effective pastors in *program* churches, *corporate* churches, as well as *mega*churches allow for the interruption and inconvenience of pastoral emergencies. They "do hospital" if only on an occasional and Spirit-selective basis. They build social capital for their leadership by repeated personal contact with persons seeking providence through the discordant elements of their lives. They speak authentic soul care language from the pulpit.

What the Rothauge analysis does accomplish is to acknowledge the naturalness of soul care in *family* congregations and *pastoral* congregations, in other words, in small churches. I would put it more strongly than that. There is a certain potential for the flourishing of soul care in the small-church setting that is lacking in other settings. The character of the church of ninety, sixty, or thirty lends itself to the maximum capacities of a pastor and of a congregation to more directly "be happy with those who are happy, and cry with those who are crying" (Rom 12:15). Small churches rely on personal contacts and quiet social contracts. They feed on face-to-face communication. They embody the maximum number of persons with whom we can have deeper relationships of sympathy, care, and communication—150 or less according to the British anthropologist Robin Dunbar.[3] Churches of larger sizes must find creative ways to replicate soul care; small churches have the favorable climate for it.

Soul Care and Stories

Soul care is the work of looking for providence in broken stories, of seeking God's presence and leadings in the rubble of a narrative collapse. There are three primary agents of that work in the small-church setting: the pastor, the congregation as active partner with the pastor, and the person receiving the care. It is a work framed by the meta stories and lesser stories of the Bible.

Chapter 3

Finding Donald

Donald (not his actual name) was a creature of habit. He always sat at the table closest to the serving line in the congregation's Wednesday evening meals for the community and toward the back of the sanctuary close to the east exit during worship. He was one of the congregation's success stories. The congregation addressed some very concrete needs for Donald: food, clothes, and repairs on his ratty old Buick as he fought to not relapse into the state of homelessness he had visited off and on in his late fifties. He found his way into our hearts with his contagious laugh, witty remarks, and disarming sincerity. And from there he found his way into our worship wearing his frayed olive sweatshirt and khaki pants. After he and I cleared the air on who was worthy and why, Donald participated in the Lord's Meal regularly and with delight. He loved the music and usually had an edgy editorial footnote to my sermon after the service. We were in conversation about his joining the church. Donald was not a "joiner" by nature, but thought he might make an exception for this congregation that cared.

Then things began to fall apart again for Donald. He was evicted from his apartment in an assisted-living complex because of numerous violations of the apartment code, which he did not dispute. Donald was a confessed hoarder. He had been given several warnings across the years and, by his own admission, just ignored them. When the exchanges with the landlord became more menacing, Donald's temper that landed him in trouble many times in the past flared up and sealed his fate. Donald was hoping to get a room at the YMCA. If not there, he would live out of his Buick, at least for the summer and fall months. The bleak prospect of becoming homeless once more weighed heavily on

50

Donald for several weeks. Who knows what part that stress and some long-term health issues played on the medical crisis that landed him in an intensive care unit of a regional medical center.

No one seems to know what happened to Donald. He was apparently alone at the time of a head injury. There was bleeding on the brain. There were seizures. By the time he was found and transported by paramedics, the lively, rascally, twinkle-in-his-eye Donald we knew was gone from us. Donald was brought to the medical center without identification. He was listed as "John Doe" for a couple of weeks. The congregation and I went looking for Donald. We tried the apartment complex from which he had been evicted, his car still parked on a street near that complex, and his friends and acquaintances. Finally, on a suggestion by one of our members I tried the area hospitals for any John Does and was able to locate Donald and give the hospital his name and the name of a family connection.

These days, Donald is cared for in a long-term nursing facility. He can sit in a chair with his eyes open, but to date there is no recognition, no speech. Our final hope is that Donald's lively soul is in the safe keeping of God. We may or may not catch a glimpse of its former self in this lifetime.

Meanwhile, we must be sure to not miss this: a congregation extended its care to a person who challenged its mostly healthy middle-class instincts about dress, responsibility, and planning. Donald in his turn was trying to learn the movements of worship, getting curious about things in the Bible, and starting to believe there was a group of persons who cared about his fate. If not for our life together in this congregation, I and the others would have had little reason or occasion to know someone like Donald. We don't cross lines of class, up or down, easily. It is a God thing when a Donald finds a church home, when his story and our story with God are mutually transformed by an updraft of providence that crosses cultures.

So Many Brothers, Sisters, Aunts, Uncles, and Cousins

Not every narrative collapse is sudden or dramatic. The loss of a family household may occur by steps over years. Children grow up and disperse. A married couple meanders into irreconcilable differences and settles on divorce. A companion of many years passes. Or a companion of many years lapses into the silence of Alzheimer's. The narrative of shared meals, holidays, memories, legends, rituals, symbols, and code words dissipates.

Outside my front door I can see the campus of a megachurch that averages 3,500 persons in worship weekly. They are a full-service church with an eighty-five-acre campus. They have athletic fields that would be the envy of some small colleges. I have served small congregations where parents with children left us for this church. The parents wanted a more complete Christian environment for their family. They wanted their children to be around other children as they learned, played, came to confession of faith, and grew into adulthood. It is a compelling logic, and I never tried to argue against it.

What I did try to do is figure out what the alternative logic might be for a small church. And I think it might be this: the small church offers a surrogate family for those whose basic family unit is dispersed or in need of wider circles of reinforcement. There are the widows and widowers who had long and good enough marriages. That social goal was achieved, that skill mastered. Now they are settled into daily patterns and a pace that suit them well. They don't want to start new complicated relationships, but they don't want to become withdrawn either. They fear being swallowed by their memories, regrets, and health issues. They know they need regular face-to-face and name recognition contact. They know they need their faith to be tangible and incarnate. They adorn the worship, ministries, and social gatherings of the small church.

√There are the empty nesters whose grown children and fast-growing grandchildren live at a distance. They keep close ties with them by hosting or traveling on holidays and vacations and by the precarious use of the latest state of social media. These empty nesters have surplus space to care for persons to whom they are not related, except by the waters of baptism and a shared Christian worldview. She has time to be aunt to the young single mother who struggles with addiction. He has time to be uncle to the young man trying to start a new business. Together they visit those of the church family who can no longer leave their residences.

There are the young single adults who obviously are just passing through on their way to life after college, military service, or the entry-level job. For a few months they lend their enthusiasm, their gifts, their surprising preference for small church and traditional liturgy. They sit alone in the pews comfortable and confident in their youth but give themselves freely in the social exchanges through which their elders soak up their energy.

Grandparents bring their grandchildren. They are not giving up on the missing generation with its casual secularity, but they would see their children's children exposed to religious faith. It is a gentle act of subversion. Those who thrive in large families where celebrations are frequent plan surprise birthday and anniversary celebrations for those who have no one else to remember. The well-dressed, bookish homeless man settles into the pew next to the family of five sporting the casual Hawaiian look.

Sometimes it occurs to me that I am witnessing the last stages of decay of a once vibrant organism, the leftovers of the heyday of nuclear families of the 1950s, '60s, and '70s, the church on its way down. I counter those gloomy thoughts by remembering some other churches on their way up, the house churches of the New Testament and first two centuries. The persons in those small churches, so to speak, come from broken homes. They answer the call to exclusive, ultimate loyalty to Jesus as Lord. It might be the catalyst for bringing to faith their entire household (Acts 16:34), but it could also mean becoming estranged from that household. We should remember one of the hard sayings of Jesus:

> His mother and brothers arrived. They stood outside and sent word to him, calling for him. A crowd was seated around him, and those sent to him said, "Look, your mother, brothers, and sisters are outside looking for you." He replied, "Who is my mother? Who are my brothers?" Looking around at those seated around him in a circle, he said, "Look, here are my mother and my brothers. Whoever does God's will is my brother, sister, and mother." (Mark 3:31-35)

In the new surrogate family of Jesus, some of the established family patterns and practices of the ancient Mediterranean are left behind such as exclusion by bloodline, firm hierarchical relations, and the limited roll assigned to women. Other patterns and practices, such as sibling solidarity, fellowship around the table, and worship, are kept but reminted to fit the members of the new surrogate family.[4]

In the Gospels Jesus builds that first surrogate community precursor to the church. First and most conspicuous, he uses familial language to address God as father (*abba/pater*) and teaches his disciples to see the father-ness of God (Luke 15:11-32) as well as the mother-ness of God (Luke 15:8-10). But within that setting, Jesus calls persons to be able to break comfortable family ties and reasonable family obligations as when he asks the two sons of Zebedee to leave their father's business (Matt 4:21-22). Jesus forms the new family to share its resources in common (Luke 8:1-3), including even burial plots (Mark 15:43, 45-46). Jesus challenges stereotypes of "a woman's place" when he welcomes Mary from the kitchen to the parlor where the men gather to hear more about the kingdom of God (Luke 10:38-42). Jesus shares the final Passover meal with his true "family" (Mark 14; Matt 26; Luke 22; John 13). He effects an adoption from the cross (John 19:25-27).[5]

The Apostle Paul opens and closes his letters to the churches with warm greetings to his many brothers and sisters in Christ. Those greetings contain glimpses of life in a surrogate family, for example, "Say hello to Rufus, who is an outstanding believer, along with his mother and mine" (Rom 16:13). Paul intervenes in local church conflicts as a parent refereeing a squabble among siblings (1 Cor 1:10) and stakes much of his authority among believers on his paternity in the faith (1 Cor 4:15; 1 Tim 4:17). He frames poor behavior in the church as a breach of family etiquette (1 Cor 1:11; 3:1; 8:11-12; 11:33; 13:11; 14:6). He coaches surrogate siblings to bear one another's burdens (Eph 6:2) and to speak the truth in love so all together may "grow" in Christ (Eph 4:15). In the most dramatic instance, he coaxes Philemon, a slave owner, to receive back the runaway slave, Onesimus, now a Christian, not as a runaway slave but as a "dearly loved brother" (Phlm 1:16).

The drama of the loss of biological and traditional family ties and the gain of new faith-based and future-oriented family ties saturates the pages of the New Testament. It is a narrative of collapse and restoration ignited by the example and lordship of Jesus Christ. And it is a staple of the soul care that can be replicated in the small-church setting.

Henry and Margaret

Henry and Margaret are in their late seventies. They left the local church over the issue of the denomination's stance on homosexuality. It was a hard loss to the small congregation. Henry is a sparkly personality who fills the room with his witty observations; Margaret has a certain elegance in her dress and manners, a quiet counterpart. They were good workers and good givers. But the denomination had just reiterated its stance that its clergy must not perform "ceremonies that celebrate homosexual unions." About the same time, the state where Henry and Margaret and their grown son who is gay live legalized such unions. As Henry put it to me when I tried to talk them out of going: "Pastor, I am ashamed of the way I apologized for my son for forty years. I've been trying to make up for it these last fifteen, and I don't have time to hang around a church that doesn't help."

On the other hand, there are other persons in the same congregation who remind me occasionally, "If the church changes its position, I'm out of here!" Some of them speak out of a persistent theology of heterosexuality grounded in their reading of scripture. Others speak out of a diffuse homophobia. Most come with some mixture of these two. The trigger for the threatened exit is usually some newsworthy protest, some act of defiance, some vocal disavowal of the church's position. The press, the social media, the advocacy groups all turn up the volume. These persons come to church primed.

But here's the thing that intrigues me about the potential of a small church to mediate social conflict and to minister to the casualties of those conflicts. The atmosphere of the small church is generally one of "time out" from the larger powers that be, whether that is the denomination flexing its muscle from above or the media in the service of breaking a social barrier. It would not be unusual for those who gather in the small church to talk as if they are fed up with "being played" by *everybody*—traditionalists, progressives, Republicans, Democrats, the connectional church, the advocacy groups, and especially the media.

Further, it would not be unusual for those persons in the small church to claim for themselves a certain freedom to stand outside the roles assigned them by the powers that be. They identify with those in the house church to whom Paul wrote his letter. "Look at your situation when you were called, brothers and sisters! By ordinary human standards not many were wise, not many were powerful, not many were from the upper class. But God chose what the world considers foolish to shame the wise. God chose what the world considers weak to shame the strong..." (1 Cor 1:26-27). They know or at least intuit that their worshipful loyalty to the God above gods releases them for independent action, especially in this place, and especially with these people.

When those who threatened to leave if the denomination changes its position asked me why they had not seen Henry and Margaret lately, I told them what Henry told me. Not one of them expressed anything but regret. It was not so much regret at Henry's position or at the church's stance, though some viewed it as a tragic necessity. For most it was regret over the absence of Henry and Margaret and regret that we all seemed to be stuck in an impossible overbearing argument that forced us to take sides.

After several persons asked about Henry and Margaret, I felt the need to share the story of their exit with the congregation at large in meetings and sermons. It elicited candid exchanges about adult children who did not feel welcome in the worship, about regrets over the guarded treatment of adult pairs in the church under the old "don't ask, don't tell" regime, and about frustration that the church could not find a way forward that made it easier to accommodate members they knew by name. It was soul care at the corporate level, the body of Christ trying to heal itself as it waited for the next move or non-move from above.

Some who want to see change in the church view the small church as the last stronghold of a rigid conservatism. That worries them because in some denominations churches of ninety, sixty, or thirty represent as many as 90 percent of the total congregations. I have more confidence in small churches than that. "It's folly they resist, not change," as David Ray so wisely observes.[6] Small churches are capable of creative, independent, and adaptive action. They are capable of working out the compromises and experiments needed to break new ground over sexuality or any other issue. They will do it in the close quarters and frequent encounters of their life together. They are not puppets waiting for the next pull of the string from above. They are agents who pray for the kingdom to come on earth as it is in heaven.

Ars Moriendi

I've witnessed the "art of dying" as a pastor in large, midsize, and small churches. I will take large and midsize any day! In those churches, the dying person's story is one attention-grabbing item among several that requires a juggler's capacity to keep them all in the air at the same time. I am not excused to give unbalanced attention to one story however gripping that story may be. For the health of the congregation at large and for my well-being as pastor of the whole people of God, I must be select in my engagements.

It is not that way in a small church. When someone is dying in our midst, for example, one who has exhausted the various protocols for cancer treatment, there is something raw and in-your-face about it. We all know the name and life story that is winding down. I am remembering Steve. We all saw his loss of weight and the worried look in the eyes of his wife, Anne. The passing of the peace was too real to pretend we didn't see what we saw. Steve tried to make us feel better by quipping about the new bald look and his stylish tossil cap.

We prayed for Steve for weeks, even months, and it became brutally apparent that our prayers were not being answered, at least not in the way we wanted. We gathered around him and anointed him with oil. We shared the medicine of the Lord's Meal with him regularly. It didn't stop the decline. This former teacher was raising questions we his pupils could not answer, questions about the efficacy of our faith.

But this is small church, so we did not try to drown out those questions, nor bypass them in our busyness. Instead, we waited and watched with Steve. And eventually he began to send us candid messages from the front. The teacher was teaching again. He told us how it feels when God says no but remains in the room as a friend. He shared accrued wisdom on the things that really matter. He cajoled us into facing our own fears surrounding death. He broke through the social censorship and talked about heaven, the communion of saints, and the resurrection life. We, the small church family left behind, agree: there was much healing and grace in the character of his exit.

Soul Care with Excellence

The small church is the natural setting for soul care, the most favorable climate to engage persons whose life stories have been disrupted and now seek God's presence and leads as they dwell among a community of persons who share a common worship, Bible, sacraments, religious calendar, building, and assorted projects of discipleship. Soul care is the work of both the pastor and the congregation in the small-church setting, but each brings distinct strengths that must be exercised with relational intelligence and from spiritual depth.

The pastor has the power of immediate access. By office and by accrued reputation the pastor does not have to wait to be invited, does not delay for the administrative assistant to arrange an appointment (there probably isn't an administrative assistant anyway), and does not overly worry about looking presentable. The pastor goes! Writers on small-church ministry sometimes talk about the charismatic nature of pastoral visitation in their settings, the freedom to set out in a car and follow the Spirit's leads as if there were some divine GPS looking out for the souls of the congregation and the community most in need of a visit.

The pastor brings a scripturally informed mind to the encounter of soul care. The pastor knows when to sit in silence and listen like Job's friends (Job 2:13) and when to enter into persons' attempts to make sense of their narrative collapses. The pastor responds in face and word, offers alternative scenarios, coaxes and cheers as the persons rewrite their life stories. And when the occasion calls for it, the pastor offers the sacramental and ritual elements of the church as tangible comfort: the bread, the cup, the oil of anointing.

The pastor remains the pastoral leader during the seasons of soul care, and that is important. In a church of ninety, sixty, or thirty, one or two serious and prolonged crises of health, finance, or family can threaten the vitality of the congregation as a corporate entity. The weight of soul care wears on the collective spirit.

One of the most important things leaders do is to help persons transcend their personal agendas for a common good. Pastoral leaders must counterbalance the weight of soul care on the congregation. They will do it first by keeping themselves as healthy and buoyant personalities. They will do it second by placing before the congregation its joys and celebrations as well as its trials and sorrows, the panoply of human experience not just one dimension (Rom 12:15). And they will do it third by weaving together in front of the congregation an interesting corporate story, The Story of Us, an ongoing subject that mitigates the isolating tendencies that cling to an individual in narrative collapse.

Members of the congregation have even more immediate access to those in need of soul care. It is worth remembering that most of the New Testament exhortations to soul care and instructions for doing it (e.g., Matt 25:31-46; James 5:13-15) are written to the members of the household of faith. And much of soul care literature through the centuries of the church is written not exclusively for or even primarily to clergy; it is written to those who have the longest history with and closest location to those needing soul care, their fellow members in the congregation.

Case in point: in a sermon first published in 1786, "On Visiting the Sick,"[7] John Wesley reminds members of the Methodist societies that visiting the sick is not only their "plain duty" according to scripture but also a "real means of grace"; in performing this work they will find their faith strengthened and their love for God and neighbor intensified.

Soul care must be practiced in person; Wesley accepts no excuses, no proxies. The power of the gospel to break down social barriers is at work in the direct contact. The rich are to visit. "One great reason why the rich in general have so little sympathy for the poor is because they so seldom visit them."[8] They should devote a set time from their daily leisure. The poor are to visit offering prayers if nothing else. The young are not too young to visit. In fact, they have "several advantages" peculiar to their station in life such as a contagious buoyancy of spirit in the presence of illness. And the old are not too old. "With what strength you have left, employ the few moments you have to spare in ministering to those who are weaker than yourselves. Your grey hairs will not fail to give you authority, and add weigh to what you speak."[9]

The everyday people of God go forth to care for their neighbors, in and beyond the community of faith, leaning on "the Giver of every good gift" for cues appropriate to the moment. There is something like a path of progression for soul care. The visitor will attend first to the outward needs of the person in physical or mental affliction, whether they have the necessities of life, the proper care, an informed diagnosis. Eventually the conversation will turn to the person's interpretation of the illness, the new narrative they must build to replace the one that collapsed. The visitor offers guided questions of general and particular providence but does not answer for the person. Sometimes the visitor will uncover a fundamental spiritual condition of acute deficit and will go to work "lovingly and gently" pressing the person toward repentance and faith in the Lord Jesus Christ. The visitor will share reading material to reinforce subjects covered.

Before leaving, the visitor will offer prescriptions of preventive care such as the value of exercise and hygiene. Wesley's visitors were supplied with a generous repertoire of these in the collection he provided for them called *Primitive Physic*. The visitor closes with prayer and makes a mental note of the subjects to follow up on at the next visit.

Chapter 4

ORDER

T here is a telling line early in the story of the books of Samuel. The people of Israel are fragile to the point of disappearance. The Philistines have defeated them in battle decisively; the casualties were in the tens of thousands. The sacred unifying symbol, the ark of the covenant, was captured. The sons of the high priest were lost in battle. And then this sad summation: "Israel was defeated, and everyone fled to their homes" (1 Sam 4:10). The corporate enterprise is finished. Or is it? The long, sometimes dramatic, sometimes subtle work of God's focused presence as Spirit must begin. And only if that occurs will this special group with a special calling to be a blessing to the nations survive and, just maybe, thrive again.

You can tell when a small church is in trouble as an organization: meetings are unfocused and unproductive not to mention poorly attended, policies and regulations are casually ignored, channels of communication are skewed, the work is conspicuously unevenly distributed, and (this is the big one) there are no plans forward. It is as if "everyone [has] fled to their homes," there to hunker down in front of state-of-the-art entertainment systems and devote themselves to lesser gods who hold fewer group expectations.

Listen to the people who leave small churches for the lift and carry of larger churches or leave church altogether. The complaints are seldom about the worship or soul care but often about the institutional life. Their spirits are worn from the friction of living in an organization that no longer does what healthy organizations do: lifts persons above their individual stories, identifies and channels gifts, adapts to changes in the regulative environment, and makes plans for a corporate future.

Lifts persons above their individual stories. Persons turn to small churches or stay in small churches because they seek more than they find home alone. Self-absorption can be a burden: a weight of cyclical thoughts, a cloying presence of regret and self-pity. The worship of a small church redirects attention upward ("I will lift up my eyes to the hills") and the engagement with others in a small church (intercessions, shared stories, side-by-side work) redirects attention outward.

This constant extroversion of persons in a small church is a marvelous work of the Spirit, an orchestration of human need and divine provision; but it can stall and even be undone when institutional order is missing. When, for example, there is no firm place to deposit anxious questions about bills not paid, employees underachieving, unsafe conditions in the building, or the need for a change in lay or pastoral leadership, the anxiety of the institution builds until it becomes a thick cloud that chokes off the search for transcendence and transcending. When meetings are "death by meeting" because the same person always tries to engineer the outcome rather than trust the wisdom reached by group consensus, or because another person keeps pausing the work of the meeting for replays of fouls committed in the dim past, or because the leader of the committee is not able to channel the meeting toward actions to be taken with accountable responsibilities assigned, when any or all of these things together happen in the corporate story of the small church, not only those engaged in the failed meetings but also those who looked to them for results become disenchanted with the life together. They are thrown back into their own stories, the ones before life together with its alleged promise of finding self by losing self in the right higher cause.

Identifies and channels gifts. The primary asset of an organization is its personnel. In for-pay organizations the gifts needed come before persons hired. There is a long and detailed process of searching, screening, selecting, and supporting. Does this person have the gift we need? In what spirit would they exercise that gift? Under what conditions would they thrive with that gift? In the volunteer organization, the persons present and available come before the gifts needed. You play the game with those who show up! This is life in a small church, and it would be a formula of desperation were it not for the promise of scripture that "you aren't missing any spiritual gift while you wait for our Lord Jesus Christ to be revealed" (1 Cor 1:7). But with that promise, those who lead in small churches and those who serve in the congregation may and should act in confidence. Somewhere among them are the gifts needed to thrive. Somehow above them the Spirit seeks to harmonize those gifts.

There is still searching, screening, selecting, and supporting to be done. And this is where the condition of the congregation's order, its administrative health, comes into play. Personnel is one of the three administrative systems in a local church, along with finances and buildings, systems that require shepherding attention and occasional courage to act. As ongoing systems, they have a certain life of their own, a native buoyancy against some mistakes and misuses. But they are not endlessly buoyant, and you don't have to be in a small church long before you pick up on neglect of personnel issues. It starts with a pastor or personnel committee pampering to the sensitivities of underperforming individuals rather than making hard decisions for the good of the body. And so, the musician, scripture reader, money counter, Sunday school teacher, and trustee who should be replaced aren't and the quality of life in the congregation seeps away slowly but surely. No folksy talk about "we're just a small church" can offset the failure to order the life of the church so that there is true alignment of gifts for the building up of the body.

Adapts to changes in the regulative environment. I teach persons how to order the life of the church, but there were parts of that life I was underestimating until I resumed the pastoral leadership of a congregation a few years ago. I went "back to the local church" only to find that the local church had not stood still at the point where I left to teach in seminary, but had moved ahead. At no place was this more evident to me than in the local church's immersion in a regulative environment. The denomination anxious about its health expected its congregations to check their vital signs weekly, especially attendance and giving. The state expected safe sanctuary training and background checks of all persons who worked with children and youth. The food bank that provided items for the weekly meal to the community expected to train the cooks and handlers and inspect the facilities. The insurance company inspected for "risk improvements" and "critical risk improvements" and expected prompt compliance on remedial action. There were tax exempt forms to be filled out and code inspections to be endured.

Larger congregations will have paid administrative persons to steer their congregations through these seas of regulation, professionals if you will. But the small church is typically made up of amateurs, persons volunteering to help the small church face the regulatory environment with some to no preparation from their workday worlds. The crucial point is that they must be *amateurs with a conscience*. That is, they must be committed to helping their congregation adapt to, not ignore or sidestep, the regulatory environment. Small churches cannot opt out of that environment. They do not exist in some transcendent plane of romanticized small-group dynamics, family-style intimacy, or organic intuition that makes such precise ordering of the life of the congregation unnecessary. The repercussions of failure to comply can be devastating: the collapse of a stairwell, the abuse of a child, the food poisoning at the community meal.

One of the nagging questions for a declining small church is this: When are we no longer a viable congregation? As we will see below, there are several strong candidates among the answers, but one of them is surely this: a small church is no longer a viable congregation when it has lost its will to adapt to its regulatory environment. When a small church has reached the point that it is not alarmed that its life together is out of compliance, morally irresponsible, or simply dangerous, it needs to summon enough courage to do one more thing right, and that is to discontinue.

Makes plans for a corporate future. Put simply: a healthy organization has a future. It claims space among other organizations that also claim their futures. It sees itself as existing a year from now, five years or ten years from now. Not every individual here and now will make it there and then, but enough will to continue the corporate story. And that projection is a significant piece of furniture in the landscape of hope for all persons here and now.

The reverse is also true: nobody wants a ride on a sinking ship. The uncomfortable feeling of many persons in small churches today is that they have bought a ticket on the *Titanic*. It may be a perception based on visible realities. Now we give up the organ we can't afford to maintain a keyboard we can. Now we give up the full-time pastor for the part-time pastor. Now we pay this bill first, then that, and third that if we have any money left. Now we are growing old together alone. Or it may be a false perception based on some outsider's criticism of the small church, a fast-moving tourist's view that misses the deeper sources of native vitality.

In either case this collective pessimism can become the controlling climate for the ordering of the life of the church. Meetings wander into nostalgia. Sighs of fatalism, of being helpless bit players in the larger storm of mainline decline, are shared around the table. Certain unpleasant facts are denied; certain hard decisions are put off. There is no talk of development. There are no plans or projections forward, only an anxious now.

The Great Campaign against Chaos

We who care, we the leaders and Spirit-gifted members of small churches, must find ways to move from resigned passiveness to confident and creative action. It is a move needed in the administration of the small church as much as it is needed in the identity, worship, and soul care of small churches. And as with those three, there is help in the biblical and theological foundations.

Original and Primary Work

It is helpful to remember that the ordering of the life of the church is original and primary work. It is not some artificial layer added onto a movement—the institutionalization (read, "corruption") of the movement called church. From its beginning the church has strived to reflect obedience to its Lord in the ordering of its life together.

When Paul says, "Everything should be done with dignity and in proper order" *because* "God isn't a God of disorder but of peace" (1 Cor 14:40, 33), he is addressing a house church, a congregation of maybe forty to fifty persons. There is tension in the gathered time for worship. Those to whom the Spirit has given the gift of speaking in ecstatic tongues and those to whom the Spirit has given the gift of prophetic messages are dominating; their overbearing behavior is detrimental to the full participation of others in worship. Those others must have complained loud enough to reach Paul through one or another of his many connections: one of those "it has been reported to me" bits of soft information Paul depends on as a leader. Now Paul intervenes with the concrete directions, directions that attempt to reconcile two energies: the raw vitality of the Spirit, its freeing impulses, and the constructive work of the Spirit, its impulses toward building up the community of faith.

Most of the basic questions of church governance or polity that still occupy our attention arose first in the life of the house churches of the New Testament. What will be the content and etiquette of our worship? Who is a candidate for baptism? How do persons become members of this community? How are disagreements handled? What are the values by which this community measures itself? What do we do with members who offend our values? Who is eligible to lead? How does the corporate body discern its next step? What is the congregation's presence in the larger community? How is this congregation connected to other congregations?

Based on scripture as interpreted through the lens of experience, tradition, and common sense, these questions are answered formally in documents written and revised periodically. The documents may be as large as a nine-hundred-page book created by an international assembly meeting every four years or as small as a ten-page covenant brought out from the filing cabinet for review at the annual meeting of the congregation.

Each local congregation interprets and applies these rules of governance as an act of discipleship. Church law is what theologian Karl Barth calls "a confessional act," a response of the community of faith to the word proclaimed.[1] It may not take liturgical form like other confessional acts such as the Lord's Meal or the Apostles' Creed, but it is an intentional public witness in written form and practice that *this* community at *this* moment will order its life together *this* way in obedience to its Lord who summons.

When someone says the small church is too small to be bothered with order; when someone rationalizes that rules, definitions, requirements, and codes were written by persons from larger churches for larger churches; when someone imagines family system dynamics can substitute for canon law in small churches; or when someone convinces the small church to trash its structure and direct all questions of order to an authoritarian pastor; that someone is blocking an original and primary expression of discipleship offered to the entire community of faith.

Steward's Work

It is also helpful to remember that ordering the life of the church is steward's work. Its biblical heritage includes God's placement of the first humans in the perfected but vulnerable garden of Eden "to farm it and to take care of it" (Gen 2:15); the extended saga of Joseph the chief steward who receives divine inspirations and follows through with shrewd and timely acts that bless his people and other nations (Gen 37–50); the parables of Jesus that contrast careless stewards to faithful stewards (Matt 25:14-30; Luke 12:41-48); and the apostles' framing of their ministry as an act of stewardship (1 Cor 4:1-2; 1 Pet 4:1, 10).

We have been entrusted with these resources in the small church: buildings we did not build (and today could not afford to), dwindling bequests from our forebears, committed volunteers and an occasional part-time staff. We have this remarkable phenomenon of a maintained weekly gathering for worship. We have the promise of the Spirit's gifts, the diversity and adequacy of those gifts. We have a self-identified community of faith, under the Spirit's tether forming and reforming itself out of obedience to its Lord and in response to changes in its environment. We have these things "in trust"; they are ours to neglect, squander, abuse; or they are ours to respect, prune, cause to flourish for a season and then hand off to the next generation.

Of the several parables Jesus told that feature stewards, one seems to have special relevance to small churches today. That is the parable in Luke 16:1-8 about a steward who mismanaged his master's resources, gets caught, and must improvise. The titles of this parable in most translations of scripture reflect the first half of the parable. The main character is identified as the unjust steward (NKJV), the dishonest manager (NRSV), or simply the crooked

73

manager (MSG). But other translations capture the turnaround in the parable; he is called the shrewd manager (GNT, NIV).

> Then Jesus said to the disciples, "There was a rich man who had a manager, and charges were brought to him that this man was squandering his property. So he summoned him and said to him, 'What is this that I hear about you? Give me an accounting of your management, because you cannot be my manager any longer.' Then the manager said to himself, 'What will I do, now that my master is taking the position away from me? I am not strong enough to dig, and I am ashamed to beg. I have decided what to do so that, when I am dismissed as manager, people may welcome me into their homes.' So, summoning his master's debtors one by one, he asked the first, 'How much do you owe my master?' He answered, 'A hundred jugs of olive oil.' He said to him, 'Take your bill, sit down quickly, and make it fifty.' Then he asked another, 'And how much do you owe?' He replied, 'A hundred containers of wheat.' He said to him, 'Take your bill and make it eighty.' And his master commended the dishonest manager because he had acted shrewdly; for the children of this age are more shrewd in dealing with their own generation than are the children of light. (NRSV)

The manager's realism about his present predicament is disarming. There is no defense or defensiveness, and not a lot of remorse for that matter, simply candor: "I am not strong enough to dig, and I am ashamed to beg." And then the leap of imagination, "I have decided what to do," which launches him into the strategy of activating dormant debts owed the master by negotiating revised terms with the debtors. The master will now recover 50–80 percent of what he is owed rather than nothing. The master commends the steward for acting "shrewdly," and Jesus says such "children of this age" have something to teach "the children of light."

✓ Shrewd stewardship is what is needed in small churches today. It begins in a clear-eyed reading of the situation. However we got here, our worship numbers are these, our financials are that, the condition of our building is such and such, the representation of generations is so and so. Then, instead of wallowing in self-pity there is the seeking for and following of inspirations for creative, adaptive action. The immediate vehicle for such inspirations may be the group under pressure in its collective wisdom or perhaps some individual who speaks more as one of "the children of this age." The final cause of such inspirations is surely the Spirit who loves this, even this church, and wants to see it flourish not flounder. /

There are small churches making shrewd decisions about the things entrusted to them, and in doing so, they insure their continued vitality. They leave behind grand buildings they cannot afford. They give up full-time clergy and staff for those who are bi-vocational. They rediscover connections with larger congregations to whom they represent themselves as a hands-on mission outpost. They find a niche ministry that makes them an asset to the community.

Heroic Work

Finally, it is helpful to remember that the ordering of the life of the church is *heroic work*. It is a visible witness to "the reconciliation of the world with God accomplished in Jesus Christ . . . the great campaign against chaos and therefore disorder."[2]

Chaos prevails when a small congregation fails to secure its continued existence in the world; but the "provisional sanctification" brought to persons through Jesus Christ is reenacted in the institution of the local church when the leadership takes steps to secure the life of the congregation and maintain its worship. Chaos has the upper hand when the community of faith is torn apart over roles, division of power, and patterns of behavior; but provisional sanctification occurs when mutual recognition, shared work, and fair treatment as prescribed in rules of governance are practiced. Chaos has the upper hand when persons leave the worship service "unfed" by the preacher and disconnected from other worshippers; but "provisional sanctification" fights back in the worship when the word is "rightly preached," the sacraments "duly administered," and the work of worship is accomplished "with dignity and in proper order" (1 Cor 14:40).

It is not a small thing to order the life of a small church, to value the corporate life of a congregation, to work for its viability and vitality. It is as close as many persons will get to influencing an institution for good and may be regarded as a Christin witness to other institutions. In the final reign of God, when the sea of chaos is no more (Rev 20:1), all institutions will reflect this commitment, fulfillment, integrity, reciprocity, flexibility, and health.

Those inside the small church must reject the dismissive remarks from outside: those who apply some metrics of organizational vitality without considering the theological "even so." The insiders must also counter talk within of an "invisible church," "the true church" that exists apart from the murky life of the institutional church. Institutional church life matters to God and is an irreplaceable theme in the story of salvation.

The hero in the heroic work of ordering the life of the small church is whoever steps forward to help the congregation name and face its challenges. There are pastors "ordained to order," meaning their calling and equipping have prepared them to inspire and pace necessary work. Those pastors serving in a small church know the people must own the work, must view it in the end as their act of faithful discipleship.

The most heroic work of ordering the life of the small church today is also the most basic: to justify its continued existence, to summon the courage to be. Chaos threatens from several directions. The constituent base has moved away. The building is showing signs of long-term neglect and lacks the amenities and appeal of newer and larger buildings. The people have grown older alone. The greater culture has become secularized. The judicatory has become impatient with the lack of growth and contribution to the greater connection of churches. Those inside the church begin to doubt the integrity of their corporate existence. They internalize the implied if not spoken criticism from outside: "Why are you still here?"

Dynamic Equilibrium

We must find a way for the small church to measure its viability and vitality that respects both the theological assurances of when church is church and the tangible factors of endurance that are there for those with eyes to see. I have experimented with the phrase "dynamic equilibrium" in recent years as a way of helping small churches find a better way of assessing their strength and making their claim to a future. The phrase was born in two experiences.

The first was an experience from above. I was serving on a bishop's cabinet with eight other persons who had supervisory responsibility for 80 to 120 churches each. This was the mid-1990s and mainline decline was no longer a debatable point. A church growth consultant was brought in, and his strategy was that we should plan for triage. Since it was "obvious" that the wave of the future was larger "magnet" churches, and since smaller churches were becoming a "drain on the system," each superintendent should identify the congregations in his or her district that had the potential to become magnet churches. The consultant determined that the current total of nine hundred churches in a conference roughly the size of central Pennsylvania should be reduced to about two hundred churches.

With the ferocity and confidence of an Old Testament prophet, the consultant forecast that in about twenty years the conference would be reduced to those two hundred churches no matter what. The issue before us was whether we as the bishop's cabinet would be passive or be proactive by favoring the two hundred above the seven hundred in the allocation of resources, time invested, and pastoral appointments.

The heart of that experience is this: we got cold feet! We held our conversations with the consultant in strictest confidence. Each superintendent had a "highly classified" list of thirty to forty congregations, the ones that would not be thrown off the boat. In our minds, and as we soon found out, in our hearts, we kept revisiting the others as if haunted by a pleading vision—"are you sure you can't keep me too?" In the end, we told the consultant, "no, thank you!" He said we would live to regret our timidity, collected his fee, and shook the dust off his feet.

We got cold feet but could not say why. We knew there was something going on there in most of those seven hundred churches "without a future" that defied our ability to name and assess accurately. One of the superintendents compared it to finding a baby bird in your yard that had fallen from its nest. You put a finger on its breast and feel a pulse. And that makes the next move ever so much more difficult.

The second was an experience from below. I have tried to grow every small church I have served, and have failed in every case but one (favored by demographics). By "grow" I mean attempting to turn it into something it was not: a midsized church on its way to becoming a larger church. There were clear signs of vitality—the character of the worship, soul care, mission, the care for its building—but there seemed to be a level above which these small churches could not go. There was something like a glass ceiling of fifty, seventy-five, or one hundred they could not crack.

These churches were not going to grow significantly larger anytime soon, but they were also not going away in the morning. Most of them had existed at about the same worship and attendance strength for several decades, a couple for a century, and one for two centuries. The individual players had come and gone, many pastors had passed through, the corporate story of the congregation continued and in all instances does to this day. How can this be?

The answer is theological and biological. The small church exists and endures because it is gathered, visited, and gifted by the Spirit to be and do church. The small church exists and endures because it is a strong Spirit-animated organism, a whole with interdependent parts pulling in the same direction, a small living system that balances its internal energies and successfully negotiates its external encounters.

Through the years I have tried to name the essential characteristics of a small church in dynamic equilibrium both to help all churches know what they have going for themselves and to help some churches assess when it may be time to disband as a congregation. The list is a little fluid because the subject of observation refuses to hold still. The most recent list has five elements.

A small church in dynamic equilibrium maintains vital worship of God. For all the reasons listed above, this is the first and foremost characteristic of a small church. The small church exists as an event that a group of persons commit themselves to on a weekly basis. The worship of God is the candle that ignites the believer's flickering faith. It brings content, focus, and direction to the forming of disciples. It sets the tone of the corporate life of the congregation throughout the week.

A small church in dynamic equilibrium provides soul care. It cares about the deepest cares of its constituents: their spiritual hungers for sure, but also worries about health, jobs, loves, losses, money. It prays for them and with them. It weeps with those who weep and rejoices with those who rejoice. And this is very important given the present demographics: it provides surrogate family for those solitary individuals or single parents seeking basic recognition and support.

A small church in dynamic equilibrium is a blessing to the community where it finds itself. Small churches participate in big causes. They participate in the appeals of the larger connection of churches, sending support for a school in India, helping to "Wipe Out Malaria!" in Africa, or organizing a work camp to a flood-devastated town in West Virginia. Observers of small churches regularly view the energy for extraversion as a key metric of sustainability.

But unlike larger churches with regional constituencies, small churches also have a more focused mandate to be connected to the narrative of the community in which they find themselves. "Promote the welfare of the city where I have sent you into exile. Pray to the Lord for it, because your future depends on its welfare" (Jer 29:7). The early narrative of most small churches was

80

intertwined with the narratives of their surrounding community around areas of education, disaster response, and public welfare and relief. The vital small church today will seek old ways and new ways to insinuate its story into the unfolding story of its vicinity.

A small church in dynamic equilibrium passes its faith to the next generation. From God's promise of descendants to Abram and Sarai to Paul's coaching of Timothy, the Bible clearly favors an intergenerational faith. "One generation will praise your works to the next one, proclaiming your mighty acts" (Ps 145:4).

Grandparents bring three-quarters of the children at our small church, and we rarely have enough children present for a group activity. The elders fear the end of the faith family line. They lament, "Where have all those young families gone?" They worry how long the "borrowed children" will want to come with "Nana and Pap." Still the elders know, we must attend to the children we *do* have, calling them by name, teaching the faith with a one-room-school model, encouraging their active participation in the worship.

A small church in dynamic equilibrium maintains its building for holy space and mission. We will explore this behavior in detail in chapter 5. A church in dynamic equilibrium attends to its properties. It employs its local indigenous religious creativity to maintain worshipful space. It is the good steward, if need be the shrewd steward in addressing obstacles to hospitality and issues of safety.

Is there something like a scaled order of regression in these elements of dynamic equilibrium? There is a certain interchangeability to items two, three, and four. A small church may have lost its connection to the community (3) but kept its children (4); or it may have lost its children (4) but still be providing soul care to the older generations (2). In my reading of the situation, the first and fifth elements are fixed. Maintaining worship (1) is the first practice to come and the last to go. Many of us know of small churches that only gather weekly for an hour of worship. It is possible but not likely that the other elements of dynamic equilibrium will return. Those churches' days are numbered.

On the other hand, maintaining a building (5) is usually the last to come and the first to go. It represents the happy moment when a vital congregation takes up a residence. It signals a strength achieved, an overflow in vitality of the people of God who have been gathering in borrowed spaces. But it is also the first and loudest indicator that a small church is in trouble. Whether it is an organ too expensive to maintain, a bell tower rendered unsafe by water damage, or simply utility bills that cannot be met, a small church overwhelmed by its building is a church at the edge of a downward spiral that threatens to pull the remaining elements of that congregation's vitality down with it.

Chapter 5

BUILDINGS

Saint Francis of Assisi is praying alone in the Church of St. Damian, a chapel that had been neglected and was in ruins. Artists who imagine the moment, show an intense wiry young man kneeling in a building with gaping holes in the ceiling and walls; the crucifix at the altar is crumbling. Francis hears a voice. "Francis, do you not see that my house is in ruins? Go and repair it."

We tend to fast-forward from that vision to Francis's life of reforming the Roman Catholic Church of his time, the early thirteenth century. "Go and fix it" is a metaphor for the bold and innovative acts that follow, such as modeling voluntary poverty, calling out the church's leaders for their negligence and abuses of power, embracing a theology of creation, and founding a monastic order.

Back up a minute. Before "go and fix it" became that grand metaphor, it was a straightforward command, one that Francis of Assisi was determined to obey. He borrowed (without asking) bales of cloth from his father's store and sold them to purchase building materials. After a public dispute with his father, the proceeds from the sale were returned, and Francis went out begging for money to buy the materials. He convinced others to volunteer their labor beside him. They rebuilt the Church of St. Damian, which became the seat of the female counterpart to the Franciscans, the Order of St. Clare. After that, Francis repaired the little church of St. Mary of the Angels and who knows how many other small churches on his way to his itinerant reform ministry.

The church is a people, but the people have always expressed their faith through the spaces they occupy and adorn. The church is a movement, but the movement always takes up physical residence. In the beginning, starting with Abram and Sarai, the people of God were "wandering Arameans" (Deut 26:5 NRSV). In the end, when the New Jerusalem descends, there will be no "temple in the city, because its temple is the Lord God Almighty and the Lamb" (Rev 21:22). But between those two endpoints the people of God have expressed their faith and found ways to support their faith in their buildings. Churchill's observation about the boomerang character of architecture ("We shape our buildings, and afterwards our buildings shape us") certainly holds true for the people of God.

In the Bible, the people of God take up residence in four buildings. First, there is the tabernacle with its portability, but also its stunning beauty, a beauty fashioned by the gifts of artistry and craftsmanship given by the Spirit to laypersons like Bezalel and Oholiab (Ex 35). Second, there is the temple built in controversy (1 Chr 17:4-14) and operated in controversy (John 2:13-25), but also providing the people of God with a house of prayer, a venue for acts of reconciliation, an experience of "the beauty of holiness," a witness to the nations, and a glimmering goal to sacred pilgrimages.

Third, there is the synagogue where God's people are gathered around God's word in anticipation of receiving inspiration and wisdom. This is the building Jesus was in the habit of visiting on the Sabbath (Luke 4:16). And fourth, there are the house churches where God's people find their native religious voice around the lordship of Jesus and form their surrogate families. They are the intimate settings for fervent worship, shared meals, listening to letters from apostles being read, and receiving guests from the growing connection of churches. When Luke says, "the Lord added daily to the community" (Acts 2:47), he is talking about the proliferation of such house churches, not the growth of a tall-steepled First Church of Jerusalem.

There are elements from the biblical heritage of four buildings in all small churches. Those who lead and those who inhabit small churches need to enter conversation with the biblical traditions, a conversation that prepares persons for responsible action. This two-step best practice, first appreciate then act, is a much-needed countermove today. It counters mere sentimentality about the building, offering instead a connection of deep feeling with faith themes. It counters those who charge that those in small churches "blindly worship their buildings," providing instead a faith perspective for loyalty to a building as well as a better faith perspective for leaving it behind—something more than the "casting down of idols." Most of all, this best practice will counter the fatalism and passiveness that many small churches have settled into regarding their buildings.

First Appreciate...

✓*Tabernacle*

Those who lead and inhabit small churches can appreciate the final portability of the worship space for God's people. The tabernacle was the focal point of the divine presence but never long in one place. The memory of the journey in the wilderness, the rhythm of setting out (in Hebrew, "pulling up stakes") and moving on at God's command (Num 33) became an enduring image of reform, of better days and a closer walk with God.

All but a handful of small churches have inhabited more than one building in the lifetime of their collective story. They have built buildings, became attached to them, and then "pulled up stakes" and moved on, usually because of growth, but also because of fire, wind, or water damage beyond repair. The moving on was a holy time, a time of grief and anxiety, but also a time for drawing closer to each other and leaning on the one who will not be contained in any house (Isa 66:1-2).

The tabernacle traditions also offer to the small church the memory of the Spirit pouring gifts upon the people for craftsmanship and artistry as they fashion the tabernacle (Exod 31:1-11). The former slaves from Egypt, whose days had been filled with the drudgery of making bricks "without straw" for Pharaoh's houses, now find themselves creating a beautiful place that would focus attention on the God who heard their cry and brought them out. Instead of the monotony of making standard-sized bricks, the ex-slaves draw blueprints, cut jewels, weave curtains, carve furniture, sew vestments, and search for oils and incense. They are even inspired to go beyond the realistic representation of objects in nature, sewing pomegranates of blue alongside those of crimson and purple (Exod 28:33; 39:24).

A small congregation's connection with its building is more immediate than that of larger churches where a board of trustees, a custodial staff, and professional contractors constitute a well-defined buffer zone between the congregation and its building.

In the small church an eighty-nine-year-old great-grandmother volunteers as custodian. The retired teacher tries his hand at a plumbing issue in the restroom. The woman who cleans for a living secures and supervises a repair by the gas company because she is chair of the trustees.

This immediacy to the building, so hands-on, so sensible, so shrewd, also has an aesthetic expression. It is given to those in a small church to fashion holy spaces and holy places in a way not given to those in larger congregations. The building they occupy is a blank canvas, and the small church paints theology on that canvas for all the world to see. They paint with the exterior of the building—the face to the community. They paint by their choices in windows and doors, pews, altar furniture, memorial adornments, as well as paintings, symbols, and other sacred artifacts.

Some of this expressed theology falls into the category of what Colleen McDannell and others call "material Christianity,"[1] the objects that believers make and buy for their homes and religious buildings, things they can see and touch that make God and the journey of faith more real. They include such things as religious china, embroidered texts and mottos, paint-by-number Da Vinci's *The Last Supper*, oversized family Bibles, bookmarks and prayer cards, funeral home advertising fans, and biblical toys and games.

These objects are often outside the sanction of the denomination or academy, but they are expressions of indigenous religious creativity and deserve their due for giving "darkness some control"[2] before being relocated or replaced. Pastors such as myself who were educated by theologians like Paul Tillich, leading us to praise Picasso's *Guernica* as sacred art and scorn Sallman's *Head of Christ* as anything but, may have some unlearning to do when serving in the small church.

Chapter 5

Temple

From the biblical temple traditions, those who lead and inhabit small churches can appreciate the importance of creating and maintaining holy spaces. The sympathetic description of the building of King Solomon's temple in Leviticus 6 includes: dating the construction as a special moment in the greater story of the people of God (v. 1); intentional choices about the play of light (v. 4); a sequenced entrance (vv. 5-6) and a sequenced ascent (v. 8) to the most holy space.

It includes the use of precious materials inside and out (vv. 7, 15, 21) and the partitioning off of an "inner sanctuary" (vv. 23-28). The building of the second temple under King Darius recalls the emotional trauma (Ezra 3:10-13) and political intrigue (Ezra 4–6) that often accompany attempts to build or rebuild sacred spaces.

Through the years I observed the attempts to create sacred space in small churches. Some are clever, some quaint. I have seen vestibules smaller than a household coat closet yet creating the sense of sequenced entry from the everyday world to the inner sanctuary. I have listened to the debates on the placing of the communion table, the pulpit, or the American flag. The arguments often lack substance[3]; but there is agreement on all sides that there is such a thing as sacred space and that there are better and lesser ways of honoring it. I have observed the awkwardness of congregations when the altar rail and even the pulpit are removed yet there remains something like an invisible electric fence to protect the altar area, however small, from undue familiarity. That awkwardness is significant; it is the vestige of a distinction crucial to spiritual health.

The Songs of Ascent (Ps 120–134) add an exterior counter-part to the temple's interior focus on holiness. The temple on a hill, like the city in which it is built, claims visual space. It inspires memories of God's intervention. "If it had not been the LORD who was on our side—let Israel now say—[our enemies] would have swallowed us up alive...the flood would have swept us away...[we would have been stuck in] "the snare of the fowlers" (124 NRSV). It broadcasts to the city and the world the secured presence of God's people in their midst. "When the Lord changed Zion's circumstances for the better, it was like we had been dream-ing. Our mouths were suddenly filled with laughter; our tongues were filled with joyful shouts. It was even said, at that time, among the nations, 'The LORD has done great things for them!'" (126:1-2). And it becomes a homing signal to those in distant places—"Oh, I'm doomed because I have been an immigrant in Meshech" (120:5)—that summons them to join their fellow pilgrims to the place where God has promised to meet them. "I rejoiced with those who said to me, 'Let's go to the LORD's house!'" (122:1). It is a place where "families live together as one" (133:1).

Our church's usually well-lit red cross was out. Al who lives eight blocks from the church was one of the first to notice. He is homebound most days but has a good view from his second-story window. He takes nightly solace in the sight of that ten-feet-high red cross that adorns the bell tower of Calvary Church as it has since February 1958. The cross marks the place where Al wor-shipped God until his debilitating stroke, the place he intends to return to someday. A neighbor was the second person to notice. "Did *they* make you turn it off?" *They* didn't, though that is an in-teresting commentary on the place of the church in contemporary society, that a person could imagine the powers-that-be ordering us to turn off our light, like the National Guard ordering a blackout during wartime.

What happened wasn't anywhere near that dramatic. A bird or something hit one of the sections of neon lights attached to the aluminum cross and shattered a section of neon tubing and a connector or two. Other parts were simply showing signs of wear. It would have taken several hundred dollars to repair the neon cross. The trustees decided it was time to replace the neon tubing with energy-efficient and easier to replace LED lights on the cross. We received donations from members and a surprising number of persons who wanted to see the cross lit even though they have no relation to the church, or perhaps any church. We lit the refurbished cross in time for the longer nights of December.

At the end of the dedication service of the original wooden cross, the congregation sang "Beneath the Cross of Jesus." The red cross is the most important symbol of Calvary's wish/prayer to be a blessing to the West Shore community. From certain vantage points it can be seen several miles away. Some have spotted it when their planes were landing at the Harrisburg International Airport. It speaks of the self-sacrificing God whose love enfolds us. It speaks of rescue and hospitality to those who stumble in the darkness. It offers direction to the lost. It summons disciples of Jesus Christ to take their stand beneath it.

Small churches make visual claims on the landscape of their communities—and they should! At their best small churches have well-kept buildings, trimmed grounds, and tended symbols that call congregants home and whisper a rumor of angels to the larger community.

Synagogue

The closest scriptural validation of contemporary small church buildings is found in the synagogue traditions. The synagogues were mostly small buildings,[4] some box-shaped with benches along the walls, some rectangular with rows of seats. The interior was very plain and could be easily converted into space for other activities such as swearing-in ceremonies, receiving charity collections, hosting community meals, and housing elementary schools.

The focus of the interior was a storage container in which was housed as many scrolls of Torah, prophets, and wisdom as could be acquired. There was a reader's lectern and lamps. Everything pointed to the primary activity: opening the scroll, reading the scripture, and expounding upon it. An inscription from the Sardis synagogue reads, "Find, open, read, observe."[5]

The Gospels tell of Jesus's participation in the weekly gatherings at the synagogue, "as was his custom" (Luke 4:16 NRSV). He formally begins his ministry at the synagogue in Nazareth, an episode that does not end well (Luke 4:16-30). Acts reports Paul's frequent visits to the synagogue where he preaches Jesus as Messiah. Some visits have good endings, some not (13:13-42, 44-50).

Surely one takeaway from the synagogue tradition for small churches is the central importance of providing a proper stage for the drama of the word read, preached, and received—creating the venue for encounters like those reported in Luke and Acts. Props and staging count: a visible canon of scriptures, not a digital slice; an intimate face-to-face arrangement of speaker and those gathered, not an isolating pulpit left over from the glory days when larger congregations required elevated speakers; and attention to light and climate control, not a fatalistic acceptance of dim and uncomfortable settings.

Advances in the study of the history of the synagogue provide a clue to a more robust small-church existence. The past scholarly consensus was that synagogues were an accommodation to exile, the people of God making due now that they were cut off from the temple. The present consensus, bolstered by new archeological evidence, is that synagogues were present before, during, and after the exile. The origins of the synagogue are obscure, but they exist from at least the third century BCE in many settings, including ones that allowed for occasional participation in the religious celebrations in the grand buildings of nearby cities, including the temple of Jerusalem.

The image is not small congregation versus large congregation, or large congregation replacing small congregation. If there was a trend, it was the springing up of small places of prayer and study of scripture alongside the larger buildings. There was the need for a more intimate encounter of persons and the word. There was also the need for larger gatherings in venues that could accommodate the pageantry, the symbolism, the large-group energy for an impactful observance of a Sabbath ritual or the festival of Sukkoth (Tabernacles). "How easily a Second Temple period Jew could move from Temple to synagogue and back again."[6]

It may suit many small churches to wear the tragic-heroic face of the synagogue in exile, to sit by the waters of Babylon, remember, and weep (Ps 137); but the image of the synagogue in concert with the temple is a better memory for small churches. Inspired by this memory, those who lead and inhabit small churches could initiate conversations with large churches, learn to honor the respective gifts of each, and experiment with an easier transport back and forth.

House Church

√ The first-century Christians gathered in the houses of their wealthier members, those with houses large enough for thirty to forty people to assemble in one room. Paul, from whom we get most of our information about the house churches, reports that was space enough for two types of activity. First, there was space in the comfort of a domestic setting for personal exchanges that increased sympathy, encouragement, accountability, and mutual recognition among the believers. Premier among these exchanges was the sharing of meals. Second, there was space to "roll up the rug" and hold corporate worship where "each one has a psalm, a teaching, a revelation, a tongue, or an interpretation" (1 Cor 14:26).

√ The house churches are the place for the gathering of the surrogate family of God, a family whose membership transcends traditional boundaries of racial identity, paternal family lines, and birthplace. It is not an invention of Paul or of the house churches themselves, but of Jesus[7] who in his ministry formed the new household of God from those he called out. "Who is my mother? Who are my brothers? . . . Whoever does God's will is my brother, sister, and mother" (Mark 3:31-35).

In the small house churches of the New Testament, members of the new surrogate family share hearts, share stuff, and mature together because they now believe that "family is more than me, the spouse, and the kids."[8] Big dramas are played out at the entrance door (Phlm 15–17). Little dramas are played out around the table (1 Cor 10–11).

A small church's capacity to offer acts of hospitality, especially space for a meal, is crucial to its purpose and continued existence. The tradition of the house church suggests a minimum standard for the necessities and amenities. Would this be okay in your home? Would you put up with something like this if you had the means to change it? Is this any way to treat your guests?

I have seen the compromises in small churches: the toilets located in a shed out back of the church, the total disregard of handicap accessibility to the indoor bathrooms, antique and uncomfortable pews, the 110-volt outlets, the impossibly steep steps, the folding chairs in disrepair, the blinking neon lights above and the yellowed asbestos floor tile below, the loose banisters and the tight doors, the climate fiascos rather than climate control, the uninviting décor. For the most part they are not items that violate building codes or fail property insurance inspections. At best, they speak of the host's shoestring budget, and at worst they speak of the host's self-absorption, a callous indifference to what could happen in that small space if it were more welcoming. Those formed by the tradition of the New Testament house churches cannot pretend they did not see what they saw.

Then Act

The resigned passivity of a small church on its way to extinction registers in its building. A cloud of fatalism hangs over it. "Whatever has happened—that's what will happen again; whatever has occurred—that's what will occur again. There's nothing new under the sun" (Eccl 1:9). The hopeful agency of a small church in dynamic equilibrium registers in its building too. The building broadcasts to dwellers, visitors, and those who pass by the virtues of stewardship, intentionality, and contemporaneity.

I have seen also small churches name and address an earlier generation's blind spots about comfort, taste, and accessibility. They get that if living in "post-Christendom" means nothing else it means small churches are not "grandfathered in" to the taste of "nones," seekers, and church shoppers. A new generation may seek fixer-uppers as potential homes or income, but not as their church. The small church that understands this will put in curb ramps, elevators, sound systems, projectors, and dropdown screens, *something, anything* to prove their intention to be taken seriously in this moment.

Hopeful small churches act as though they are not captive to an earlier generation's sense of sacred space. What constitutes sacred space changes. Many small churches have lived through at least three versions of sacred space with their respective messages: Akron, divided chancel, and open stage. Each has strengths and weaknesses, each its theological messages and its attempts to accommodate the present age. The pressing question for the small church is not which is the correct version for all time, but how shall this generation arrange its furniture to convey sacred space? It assumes a local power and creativity to act. It feeds on a conviction that God's epiphanies are not a thing of the past.

Nor are these small churches captive to an earlier generation's sacred artifacts. Some of the artifacts may transcend the changing tastes of generations to become permanent fixtures in the congregation's longer story. In my area where there are many persons of German descent, Heinrich Hofmann's *Christ in the Garden of Gethsemane* is a staple of older small churches. But other artifacts have lost their power to convey their intended message: the

oversized oil-burning chandelier that can't be used, the pulpit
Bible in a translation nobody understands, the dimly lit sign out
front with gothic letter font impossible to read. Some artifacts
have become an obstacle to the congregation's experience of the
holy, others an obstacle to its communication to the community.
The pressing question is not one of aesthetics, but agency. Once
we finally name the elephant in the room, how do we get it out?

The Special Case of a Small Church in an Oversized Building

There is a stereotypical empty church scene in movies and
television shows today. The lead actor, like Macaulay Culkin in
Home Alone (1990), is dwarfed by row upon row of empty pews.
He sits alone or in quiet conversation with another solitary visitor. They are awash in the warm ambience of lowered lights and
several candles. If there is activity at the distant altar area before
them, it is only a choir practicing softly or someone praying. The
scene speaks of sanctuary and recovered focus, of being still and
getting things straight.

I am the pastor at this church building and so are many others
who are serving congregations where only ninety, sixty, or thirty
people gather together for worship on Sunday morning in sanc-
tuaries that could seat 500, 750, 1000, or more. Speaking for my
colleagues, we are mostly avid fans of those empty church scenes
in the movies or TV. We like to re-create them for others, perhaps
leaving the empty sanctuary unlocked more than we should. We
like to experience these scenes ourselves—so natural to talk to
God there, so easy to recall the faces of God's people past and
present.

But speaking for those same colleagues, the warm scene also gives off the scent of leaves decomposing, of living things that have gone beyond the point of return. It is a constant reminder of a seemingly impossible situation. I offer the following case study not because it is special, but because it is all too typical. It is being played out in cities and towns, wherever small congregations struggle under the weight of their oversized buildings.

I came to Calvary United Methodist, Lemoyne, Pennsylvania, in my favorite pastoral role, as one who rescues. My predecessor simply quit on the third Sunday of Advent, announcing his decision to the congregation and his supervisor via a group e-mail. A few months after my pastorship began, there was a settling down and a settling in. The attendance started to come back. The bills got paid. The depressed spirit of the congregation lifted and a more buoyant, friendly one took its place. After three years, we began to plateau. Those of the former congregation who could "come back" had, and we were not connecting with enough visitors to generate a new constituency of support. Younger worshippers would visit once, look around, mumble something polite after the service, and disappear.

Calvary was once a vibrant seven-hundred-member congregation with two full-time ordained pastors, a staff of eight, and an average weekly worship attendance of 338 (1963). Calvary was a "big church" and had the building to prove it. Its 20,500 square feet of enclosed space was built in two phases, the main sanctuary in 1906 and an adjacent fellowship hall in 1958. It embodies the Romanesque Revival style with its fortress-like exterior, towers, heavy brick walls, and arches over the windows and doors. Its five stained glass windows are valued at $300,000, the pipe organ at

$200,000. The replacement value of the rest of the building is $5,280,000.

Through the decades of mainline decline, Calvary declined too but at a gentle rate. Leaders and members made necessary adjustments. The staff was reduced in number and then transitioned from full-time to part-time. Clergy presence was reduced from two full-time, two part-time, to one full-time, and then, with my coming, one part-time. When the financial commitments to the connectional church and missions were at risk, the congregation drew down its savings and kept faith. They learned to live within their means. Yet at the same time the 110-year-old building continued to exert its claims at a rate that was becoming irritating and eventually alarming.

In my first year at Calvary we had to address two critical risk recommendations from a recent insurance inspection: jersey barriers for a parking lot near the nursery school ($3,000) and a ventilating hood for the twenty-burner gas oven ($21,000). Year two the air conditioning unit gave out ($20,000) and the dreary lighted sign in front demanded replacement ($5,000). Year three we filled and patched the sinkholes in the 12,500 square-foot parking lot ($11,000) but held off on the resurfacing ($30,000) that would have completed the job. In year four we rescued the red cross on the State Street tower ($6,000) and replaced some very old gas pipes that were beginning to leak ($4,000) in the boiler room. One of the trustees reminds me the boiler pipes, and cast-iron radiators have lasted much longer than we have a right to ask (estimated cost $42,000). The organist reminds me that the "leaking expression shades" need repaired soon ($29,000) and a hole in the "blower reservoir" needs repaired now ($4,000). "Should I start to play the hymns at the piano?"

At one point in year four I tried to take us on the offensive. I convinced the leadership to hire an architect and draw up plans for a welcome center. The renovated restrooms, infant care room, and coffee serving area would be near the entrance of the sanctuary. It would surely give us the $64,000 makeover we needed to hold the younger visitors. The congregation was cautiously positive. Some, but not enough, pledged financial support. In the end, I was the one to pull the plug. I could not in good conscience put them in a debt that would likely hasten death.

So here we are: loving our tabernacle, temple, synagogue, house church, but not able to afford it. We cannot improve items of décor, comfort, or convenience. We are waiting for the next large-ticket item that will empty our savings or drastically change our lifestyle, such as giving up the organ for the piano or closing off part of the building.

It is an unfinished story with a probable finish. And the finish is that Calvary Church will do what dozens of formerly large churches have done in the city where we are located and thousands have done across the country. They will gather on the deck of the *Titanic* to sing "Nearer My God to Thee" as it goes down. That is, they will exhaust their last spiritual gifts for ministry, their last impulses to form surrogate family, their last bit of confidence that they have a message the community needs, exhaust them for the lesser cause of keeping their building open as their numbers dwindle. Last one out, turn off the lights!

As their pastoral leader, my strong desire is that Calvary would avoid that probable finish. They deserve better than the pall of fatalism that settles over a disappearing congregation in an oversized building. To that end I have asked the leaders and congregation to join me in three actions.

Accept that we are a healthy small church rather than a sick larger church. This is not easy for anyone who remembers the glory days nor for the pastor who wants to be the hero who brings them back; but it is the crucial first step to survival. If we seek new constituents to breathe life into a larger church, our efforts will be desperate and will come across that way. Come fill our seats, our offering plate, our fading programs! On the other hand, if we rest in our strengths as a small church—and there are many—our invitations can be spontaneous. We are not recruiting; we have something good to give away to those who may be receptive.

Face the reality of our oversized building. Sometimes the elephant in the room is the room! We need to keep talking about the mounting and impossible demands of the building. For nearly fifty years in ministry I have been waiting for the anonymous widow to surprise everyone by leaving the church a million dollars at her death. It has yet to happen! I count the rich widow's gift among the many fantasies that distract God's people from taking necessary action. Frank talk about limiting and even dangerous conditions in the building forces the congregation to ask after its core identity.

Before it is too late, decide for the people of God over the present building. We're not there yet at Calvary. If we abandon 700 Market Street now, we lose precious worship ambience and the capacity for two vital ministries. But that day may be coming. I try to remember that any given congregation has outlived at least two buildings, some nearly a dozen. Every church knows what it is to pick up stakes and move on. Calvary was started as a prayer meeting in a lawyer's office across the street from its present location. It is not that buildings don't matter; they do for all the reasons specified above. But when it comes down to choosing between a vital congregation in dynamic equilibrium or squandering the resources of that congregation to maintain an oversized building, the God of Abraham (Gen 12:1-7) should win out every time.

Chapter 6

A SIGNIFICANT CHURCH

I have my Feuerbach moments, those dark and gloomy hours when the father of the Masters of Suspicion (Marx, Nietzsche, Freud) takes up residence inside my head. He chants the well-worn phrases of the projection theory of religion. God is only the human person idealized and imagined as an external object. Providence and prayer are desperate wishes that humans can be exempt from their external circumstances. Trinity is a metaphor for the human struggle to synthesize reason, will, and emotion. Heaven is an understandable attempt to deny the grim reality of one's own death.

And the church? The church is a collective egocentric illusion, a prejudice that our group is a special group. It has its origin in Judaism with its twin doctrines of a special creation and the call of a chosen people. Through the centuries Christians blamed the Jews for their "most narrow-hearted egoism," but did not hesitate to transfer that egoism to themselves in the doctrine of the kingdom of God to which many are called but few chosen.[1]

Is that what is going on here in the small church? Are we the gathered and sent people of ninety, sixty, or thirty being seduced by a collective egocentric illusion? Are we running from unpleasant truths, truths like our insignificance in the grand scheme of things or our vulnerability to the winds of fortune? Are we fabricating stories like our need for worship to project purpose into our empty lives, or stories about our Spirit-giftedness to compensate for losses in the real world of work and recognition? And are the compromises of the small church—its part-time clergy, its cramped buildings or its oversized buildings, and its almost total dependence on volunteerism—an especially desperate and conspicuous example of the collective egocentric illusion? In the brooding, skeptical presence of Feuerbach and anyone else who would dismiss the small church as "nothing but...," I ask these questions.

Is the Small Church You Talk about a Fiction?

I have spent years dissing one fiction about small churches—that of nostalgia. It is deadly for a small church to see itself trapped in an idealized past. Even the Little Brown Church in the Wildwood must seek contemporaneity with God and neighbors.[2] Have I simply created another fiction in its place, one based on a handful of biblical expressions such as people of God, body of Christ, the call to worship, spiritual gifts, and good order? Have I sprinkled the dull oatmeal of an aging, shrinking, and failing religious enterprise with the sugar of theological catchphrases such as Spirit-animated organism, indigenous religious creativity, surrogate family, and dynamic equilibrium?

The answer is, of course, yes! I have created a fiction of the small church. It is a fiction of love, fabricated from the Bible and amplified from the church's theology, especially ecclesiology. And as a leader of a small church I maintain this fiction, nourish it, and place it out in the public space to claim a space and bump up against the other competitive fictions about the small church.

We all start from the same data: the people and their activities; their corporate story; the space they occupy; the trajectories of size, age, and composition; their footprint in the community. Some take that data and create stories with plots like "survival of the fittest," "drain on the connection of churches," "church is not a building," or "nothing but a relic on the religious landscape."

I take that data and create a fiction about a significant church, one able to be everything a church can be and do everything a church should do. In my story that church worships God, provides soul care, orders its life together, stewards its building, blesses its community, and passes its faith to the next generation. It embodies the six marks of "true church": one, holy, catholic, apostolic, where the word is preached rightly, and the sacraments are practiced regularly. It sings its songs of deliverance (Ps 124); its angel hovers over it (Rev 1–3).

One thing has become very clear to me in recent years. I was not capable of discovering or maintaining a hopeful vision for the small church on my own. I was equipped for it by my theological education. I served a small church while in college. Lucky for me and for them, the church as a whole was healthier in those days. There were many mistakes! I was especially lacking in the emotional intelligence skills that I teach as essential to church leadership today. Yet the church was resilient and had no pressing need for apologetics, for someone to tell them who they were before God and why they mattered to the community. Times have changed and the tolerance for poor leadership in a small church is almost zero.

I was taught the language and ideas I have needed to weave a vision of hope for small churches in seminary. No seminary, no power to talk back to the lesser fictions about the small church. It's that simple. I point this out to challenge the prevailing fallacy that an educated clergy is essential for larger churches but optional for small ones. It takes an MDiv or some comparable form of robust theological education to provide the leadership that small churches need today.

How Serious Can You Be with a Part-Time Pastor?

I have never led/served a small church with undivided attention. Nor have most of the pastors of small churches I have known. Even when we were in full-time ministry, our attention was divided among two, three, or more congregations. The congregations typically had little affinity. Often they were duct-taped together by the judicatory to create a full-time salary package.

I have led/served several churches in a full-time capacity and recognize the difference. Here there is greater focus on the other, longer and more consistent periods of attention, the playful redundancy of information from which good decisions come, the possibility of establishing a rhythm of being down on the dance floor and up on the balcony.[3]

One of the brightest moments in the life of a small church is when it has grown enough to have "our own pastor." One of the bitterest disappointments, "shame" would not be too strong a word, is when a midsize church on the way down must begin to share its pastor. I came to Calvary of Lemoyne on the slope of that second scenario. After more than one hundred years of having an ordained full-time pastor (for three decades, two full-time pastors), Calvary could no longer afford the salary, insurance, and pension for a full-time pastor. It was a marriage of convenience. I had recently cut back my work at the seminary and was seeking to, as I put it, "get back into preaching."

I began work at quarter-time, then moved to half-time, and finally three-quarter-time. I told Calvary at the start that my immediate goal was to build them up to the point where they could have their own full-time pastor again. It was a foolish thing to say on two accounts. First it totally underestimated the depth of their decline as measured in families lost, financial resources maxed out, and deferred maintenance on the building. And second it labeled my leadership as inferior and hopefully temporary. As Calvary settled in for the long haul of rebranding itself as a small congregation, there was yet another piece of the glorious past to be left behind: the prestige and attention of a full-time pastor. And as I settled in for the long haul of leading Calvary, I knew I had some rebranding to do as well.

Quarter-time, half-time, and *three-quarter-time* are terms gathered from the secular workplace and refer primarily to hours of labor specified in a contract. They are a useful, if not always desired, distinction for purposes of limiting hours worked and compensation received.

In the image of the Apostle Paul as the tentmaker missionary (Acts 18:1-4), we are given an alternative perspective on the church leader who devotes less than full-time attention to a ministry. This church leader deliberately chooses to work with his hands in a trade (Acts 20:34-35; 1 Cor 4:12; 2 Cor 11:27; 1 Thess 2:9; 2 Thess 3:8). Paul is equipped by education and worthy by hours invested to be fully funded for the work of ministry. Instead he chooses to support himself and his traveling companions by working in the trade of making tents. It is hard work, "working day and night," working in the close quarters with other laborers, including slaves. There is the noise and grime of a shop, the dearth of light, the hours of mind-numbing repetitive acts of manipulating leather with knives, awls, and needles.[4]

Why would Paul choose this way of doing ministry? There are at least three reasons. First, Paul has a strong work ethic grounded in his mastery of a trade. He takes pride in his work and enjoys the confidence and self-sufficiency it provides. In fact, he can be harsh with those who do not share his work ethic. "If anyone doesn't want to work, they shouldn't eat" (2 Thess 3:10). Second, Paul has discovered that certain work settings will afford him opportunities to share his faith, not as a religious professional but as a fellow worker. He spends the best hours of the day in a place where his skills and work ethic garner respect and open ears (tentmaking is one of the quieter trades) to receive his remarkable stories of Jesus, his enemy turned Lord. Third, Paul wants an independence from the congregations (1 Cor 9:15-18). He would not be beholden, but would retain the purity of his commission. He cherishes a capacity to say what must be said to the church, a freedom to speak the truth in love. The pastor of the small church who also drives a school bus, sells insurance, teaches school, or holds a paid political office may come to appreciate any or all of Paul's reasons.

I would add a fourth reason. The pastor as tentmaker may experience a "spillover effect." The phrase can be used negatively as when one person's bad mood affects others, but also can be used positively as when an advance in the NASA space program becomes a blanket for marathon runners at the end of the race. Something in one context has an impact for good in a completely unrelated context. I don't know if Paul ever experienced the spillover effect, but I and many of the tentmaker pastors of my acquaintance have.

Before Clementa Pinckney became a martyr to the cause of racial harmony, he was a quiet student in the doctoral program at Wesley Theological Seminary where he was studying that spill-over effect. Clementa was living in two worlds separated by a long commute, Emanuel AME Church in Charleston and the South Carolina Senate in Columbia. He was successful in both worlds but nagged by the question of whether he could have even greater impact were he to choose one over the other.

At the same time, he knew there was a tradition of bi-vocational African American pastors who were called to stand in a second world of work outside their congregations and in fact seemed to draw energy from the traveling back and forth. Clementa was writing about Paul the apostle/tentmaker and Richard Allen the preacher/businessman at the time of his death. No one other than the senator would appreciate more the irony of events that unfolded after June 17, 2015, the day he and eight other African Americans were shot and killed in their church while attending a Bible study: the flag came down in Columbia, an unfinished national conversation about race was resumed, and extraordinary acts of human compassion were ignited. All because the pastor kept to his Wednesday evening practice of conducting a Bible study to which all were welcome.[5]

What If You Are on the Wrong Side of History?

The History of This Local Congregation

Last Sunday morning the worship service caused me to wonder if Calvary is in a freefall. Our attendance has been down by twenty to thirty persons most of the month of January. Weather, sickness, snowbirds to be sure, but also troubling signs that we have reached some tipping point. So many of our actives have become shut-ins over the last few months. It sometimes feels as though the shut-ins will outnumber the worshipping congregation soon. There are so few new faces checking us out. There hasn't been a confession of faith in four months, an infant baptism in over a year. There are persistent complaints from the clients of both of our rental incomes. The organ has a noticeable wheeze. The one place where we seem to be growing is in the number of persons, many of them quite desperate, whom we serve in our food, clothes, and other supportive ministries. To add imagined insult to imagined injury, if the worshipping congregation goes, so do these ministries!

Having seen the deaths of many small churches in my years of ministry, I know that as with persons so with institutions: there are good deaths and not so good deaths, peaceful deaths and agitated deaths. The decisive factor is a compassionate and informed leader. One pastor applies the wisdom accrued from her first career in hospice to help the congregation become more active agent than passive victim through the waning days. Another pastor guides his congregation in the process of writing and celebrating a defined "completion" to its corporate story. Still another guides his congregation through the process of accepting its life cycle and planning a legacy.

I know what a dying small church looks like, and Calvary is not there yet. There may be a death we do have to face: our death as a large church. More particularly, our death as a congregation capable of sustaining our grand building. If that day comes, my hope is that we can reset our self-image and recalibrate our expectations. I would have us live into the dynamic equilibrium of a healthy small church that maintains vital worship of God, provides soul care, blesses its community, passes its faith to the next generation, and maintains a *smaller building* for holy space and ministry.

The History of This Local Community

You hear this lament in three moves in many small churches today: We were created to share the gospel with an underserved population. The population moved on. We didn't. The lament may be heard in rural settings where agribusiness has depleted the clusters of population from whom the small churches drew. The migrant workers don't have time; the undocumented workers keep a weary distance. It is also heard in urban settings where small congregations gather in ancient oversized buildings that are dwarfed by urban redevelopment projects. The congregation is sustained by a nonresident population in their eighties or nineties. They will soon lose their driver's licenses.

Calvary's version of that lament includes this undeniable change: the community that was once a residential community of churchgoing families with two to five children, and bread-winners who worked for the state or the many businesses thriving in the economy of the state capital, has become, per the census, a community of renters, with poverty "significantly above" the state average,[6] where half the households are single-parent, and the fastest-growing religious preference is None.

The prognosis for our ministries of food, clothing, and other support looks good; the prognosis for growing a strong congregation to maintain those ministries not so much. The dissonance causes soul searching. If we abandon our oversized building for a rightsized one, where should that building be? There are certainly better demographics for growing churches. If we were church planters we would look to the fields that might yield more abundant harvests. But we are not church planters; we are church, and we are located at a place where we can do a lot of good.

Our occupied and well-kept building supports community property values. Our ministries meet real needs of persons of the community not otherwise helped. Our gathering and scattering under our pregnant symbols like that lighted red cross create a foothold for transcendence in the community that otherwise might think itself comfortably secular. God? Well, maybe.

The History of Mainline Decline

The most pressing theological issue of my lifetime turned out to be none of the great headline-grabbing controversies of my young-adult years: Death of God, Passover Plot, Lost Gospels. The most pressing theological issue has been the loss of vitality of the mainline church in which I was baptized, came to faith, and followed a call to ministry. That decline, which is now measured at five decades or more, continues to register from congregations to seminaries, from church-related institutions to judicatory services, from the condition of buildings to pastoral support.

The decline of mainline churches has brought the nature and mission of the church front and center. We are in a season of intense questioning. Did Jesus intend the church of all-too-human disciples? How does the church respond to its disestablishment? What is the value of the local church as it rides out the conflicts and evolving phases of its denomination? How shall congregational vitality be measured? Where does real church happen?

Some see small churches as a part of the problem. They judge their size as a business enterprise that never quite took off; small churches have not carried their weight. They know that many small churches today are failed midsize and even large churches of yesterday. They hear that on any given Sunday 50 percent of worshippers are in the 10 percent of larger churches and the trend is growing. They watch small churches scale back in their leadership: now an ordained pastor, now a local pastor, now a certified lay speaker, now an uncertified one. As goes the mainline, so goes the small church.

I prefer to see small churches as part of the solution. In the first place these "failed enterprises" have been around a long time. They have replenished themselves with new players and new services for decades, and in some cases centuries. That's a durability worth pondering. They have survived the rumbles and trendy phases of their denominations. Those that were formerly larger may have found a new dynamic equilibrium, a reset that breaks the fall and allows them to write a new chapter of the congregational story.

Small churches have a quiet but diffuse witness to share with congregations of all sizes. It is a witness to the value of maintaining focus over the long run, of being thrown again and again on the Spirit for buoyancy and gifts, of being shrewd in dire circumstances. It is a witness to the worth of being a place where everyone knows your name and all together call upon the name of the Lord and thereby experience more abundant life.

NOTES

1. An Exercise in Selective Amnesia

1. Stanley Hauerwas and William H. Willimon, *Resident Aliens: Life in the Christian Colony* (Nashville: Abingdon Press, 1989), 15–19.

2. "Calculators: Life Expectancy," Social Security Administration, accessed June 7, 2016, www.ssa.gov/planners/lifeexpectancy .html.

3. *The American Heritage College Dictionary*, 4th ed., s.v. "caricature."

4. Walter Chambers Smith, "Immortal Invisible, God Only Wise," *The United Methodist Hymnal* (Nashville: The United Methodist Publishing House, 1989), 103.

5. Dietrich Bonhoeffer, *Life Together: The Classic Exploration of Faith in Community*, trans. John W. Doberstein (New York: HarperOne, 1954), 26–30.

6. See Graig Van Gelder, *A Community Led by the Spirit: The Ministry of the Missional Church* (Grand Rapids: Baker Books, 2007) for a helpful version of this list that traces its biblical and historical expressions and argues for its relevance to a contemporary reformation of the church.

7. Romans 12:6-8; 1 Corinthians 12:7-11, 27-31; Ephesians 4:11-12.

2. Maintaining Worship

1. Thomas Edward Frank, *The Soul of the Congregation: An Invitation to Congregational Reflection* (Nashville: Abingdon, 2000).

2. George Croly, "Spirit of God, Descend upon My Heart," *The United Methodist Hymnal* (Nashville: The United Methodist Publishing House, 1989), 500.

3. Charles Wesley, "Spirit of Faith, Come Down," *The United Methodist Hymnal* (Nashville: The United Methodist Publishing House, 1989), 332.

4. Afro-American spiritual, "I'm Goin' a Sing When the Spirit Says Sing," *The United Methodist Hymnal* (Nashville: The United Methodist Publishing House, 1989), 333.

5. Fred Kaan, "Help Us Accept Each Other," *The United Methodist Hymnal* (Nashville: The United Methodist Publishing House, 1989), 560.

6. A history of the birth of small churches will credit the clergy and connections that sent them to found new congregations, but also will include the story of the lay movements that gave rise to new congregations, movements such as German pietism, Methodist societies, the Sunday school movement, lay ecclesial movements (Roman Catholic), and various house church or simple church movements.

7. Larry W. Hurtado, *Lord Jesus Christ: Devotion to Jesus in Earliest Christianity* (Grand Rapids/Cambridge, U.K.: William B. Eerdmans, 2003; paperback edition, 2005), 1–11.

8. Ibid., 29–52.

9. Ibid., 138–53, 179–88.

10. Sydney Carter, "Lord of the Dance," *The United Methodist Hymnal* (Nashville: The United Methodist Publishing House, 1989), 261.

11. Ibid.

12. Ibid.

13. Anne Lamott, *Help, Thanks, Wow: The Three Essential Prayers* (New York: Riverhead Books, 2012).

14. For a discussion of these practices in a small church setting, see Lewis A. Parks, *Preaching in the Small Membership Church* (Nashville: Abingdon, 2009), chap. 4.

15. John Wesley, "The Preface" in *The Works of John Wesley, Volume 1, Sermons 1 (1–33),* ed. Albert C. Outler (Nashville: Abingdon Press, 1984), 103–5.

16. The efforts of individual theologians (e.g., John Calvin, Paul Tillich, Michael J. Rose) and judicatories (e.g., "Built of Living Stones: Art, Architecture, and Worship" by the United States Conference of Catholic Bishops) to distinguish between good taste and poor taste in congregational life are helpful, but so also is the reminder by Colleen McDannell, Deborah Sokolove and others that the tension between officially sanctioned beauty and indigenous visual expressions of religious faith is a two-way street at best and a quenching of the Spirit at worst. See Colleen McDannell, *Material Christianity: Religion and Popular Culture in America* (New Haven & London: Yale University Press, 1995), 1–16, 163–97; Deborah Sokolove, *Sanctifying Art: Inviting Conversation between Artists, Theologians, and the Church* (Eugene, OR: Cascade Books, 2013), 65–97.

17. It is the heritage of the Quadrilateral (scripture interpreted through the lens of tradition, reason, and experience), of John Wesley's creative uses of the empiricist epistemology of John Locke, of the mutual sharing in class meetings, of the salvation "applied to me" twist of Charles Wesley's hymns, of the lay class leaders turned preachers, and of the deathbed accounts published in *Arminian Magazine.*

18. *The Book of Discipline of The United Methodist Church 2012,* eds. L. Fitzgerald Reist, Neil M. Alexander, and Marvin W. Cropsey (Nashville: United Methodist Publishing House, 2012), 23.

3. Soul Care

1. Arlin Rothauge, *Sizing Up a Congregation for New Member Ministry* (New York: Episcopal Church Center, 1983).

2. Ibid., 9, 12, 17–20, 26–27.

3. Robin Dunbar, *Grooming, Gossip, and the Evolution of Language* (Cambridge, MA: Harvard University Press, 1996), 69–77. "Dunbar's number" is the maximum number of persons with whom we can have significant relationships because of our cognitive limits, the way our brains are wired. He argues for 150 or less as the ideal size of community and illustrates from ancient clans, modern villages, small businesses, military units, and congregations.

4. Joseph H. Hellerman, *The Ancient Church as Family* (Minneapolis, MN: Fortress Press, 2004), chap. 2–3. Hellerman compares and contrasts the surrogate families of the ancient church with professional organizations like trade groups, cult associations, philosophical schools, and the Jewish synagogues. He finds the small Christian faith communities conspicuous at the points of being trans-local, socially inclusive, structurally egalitarian, opposed to the dominant culture, and having a strong family emphasis.

5. Ibid., 67.

6. David R. Ray, *The Indispensable Guide for Smaller Churches* (Cleveland, OH: Pilgrim Press, 2003), 112.

7. John Wesley, Sermon 98: "On Visiting the Sick" in *The Works of John Wesley, Volume 3: Sermons 3 (74–114),* ed. Frank Baker (Nashville: Abingdon Press, 1986), 385–97.

8. Ibid., 387.

9. Ibid., 394–95.

4. Order

1. Karl Barth, *Church Dogmatics* IV/2, ¶67.4, 682, 707.

2. Ibid., 676.

5. Buildings

1. Colleen McDannell, *Material Christianity: Religion and Popular Culture in America* (New Haven & London: Yale University Press, 1995), chap. 1, 6.

2. From Robert Lowell's poem "Waking Early Sunday Morning" (1967).

3. They are not given much help. When mainline denominations were growing, they routinely offered resources, even dedicated staff, to assist local churches with their buildings. They offered that help to churches of all sizes. Today those resources, like the Bureau of Architecture of the Methodist Episcopal Church, which offered consultation, plans, and publications like *Rebuilding the Town and Country Church* (1928), have dried up, tempting small churches with less resources to fast-forward past any theological reflection before acting on their buildings.

4. Although excavation has uncovered a few larger synagogues like the great synagogue at Sardis that could contain one thousand persons, the normal size is much smaller. For example, from the second temple period, the synagogue near Modi'in measures 39 x 33 feet; the Kiryat Sefer synagogue measures 31 x 31 feet, and the Masada synagogue measures 30 x 30 feet! Steven Fine and John David Brolley, "Synagogue" in *The New Interpreter's Dictionary of the Bible* (Nashville: Abingdon, 2009).

5. Ibid.

6. Ibid.

7. Jesus practices but amps up a pattern that can be found in some Old Testament texts (e.g., Gen 12:1-3; 22; Deut 13:6-9; Isa 60:1-3) of appreciating family ties and obligations while projecting those benefits beyond one's biological kin based on a call or vision from God. Joseph H. Hellerman, *The Ancient Church as Family* (Minneapolis, MN: Fortress Press, 2004), 59–70.

8. Joseph H. Hellerman, *When the Church Was a Family: Recapturing Jesus' Vision for Authentic Christian Community* (Nashville: B&H Publishing Group, 2009), chap. 7.

6. A Significant Church

1. Ludwig Feuerbach, *The Essence of Christianity*, 2nd ed., trans. George Eliot (1881; repr., Mineola, NY: Dover Publications, Inc., 2008), 93–100, 247.

2. As it clearly does. See The Little Brown Church in the Vale, accessed January 26, 2017, www.littlebrownchurch.org.

3. Ronald A. Heifetz, *Leadership without Easy Answers* (Cambridge, MA: Belknap Press of Harvard University Press, 1994), 252–54.

4. Ronald F. Hock, *The Social Context of Paul's Ministry: Tentmaking and Apostleship* (Philadelphia: Fortress, 1980). This groundbreaking work remains the jumping-off point for the exploration of this peculiarity of Paul's ministry style.

5. Clementa C. Pinckney was awarded the doctor of ministry degree posthumously at the Wesley Theological Seminary Commencement, May 7, 2016.

6. "The FullInsite Report," prepared for Lemoyne, Calvary, accessed February 21, 2017, https://maps.missioninsite.com /Generatefile.aspx?Type=3&ID=569359.

CPSIA information can be obtained
at www.ICGtesting.com
Printed in the USA
LVOW13s0555280317
528667LV00003B/4/P